Atomic Productivity

Train Your Brain to Like Doing Hard Tasks Without Exhausting Your Self-Discipline Through Behavior Hacks and Small but Lasting Habits

Leo Black

© Copyright 2020 - All rights reserved.

The content contained within this book may not be reproduced, duplicated or transmitted without direct written permission from the author or the publisher.

Under no circumstances will any blame or legal responsibility be held against the publisher, or author, for any damages, reparation, or monetary loss due to the information contained within this book, either directly or indirectly.

Legal Notice:

This book is copyright protected. It is only for personal use. You cannot amend, distribute, sell, use, quote or paraphrase any part, or the content within this book, without the consent of the author or publisher.

Disclaimer Notice:

Please note the information contained within this document is for educational and entertainment purposes only. All effort has been executed to present accurate, up to date, reliable, complete information. No warranties of any kind are declared or implied. Readers acknowledge that the author is not engaged in the rendering of legal, financial, medical or professional advice. The content within this book has been derived from various sources. Please consult a licensed professional before attempting any techniques outlined in this book.

By reading this document, the reader agrees that under no circumstances is the author responsible for any losses, direct or indirect, that are incurred as a result of the use of the information contained within this document, including, but not limited to, errors, omissions, or inaccuracies.

Table of Contents

INTRODUCTION 1

CHAPTER 1: THE PREMISE OF PRODUCTIVITY 3

   THE DEFINITION OF PRODUCTIVITY 4
   MEASURING PRODUCTIVITY 5
      Setting Measurable Objectives 6

CHAPTER 2: WHAT PREVENTS PRODUCTIVITY 11

   PROCRASTINATION 11
      Why It's a Problem 12
      How to Fix It 13
   CELLPHONES AND NOTIFICATIONS 14
      Why It's a Problem 15
      How to Fix It 15
   EMAILS 17
      Why It's a Problem 17
      How to Fix It 18
   CLUTTER 20
      Why It's a Problem 20
      How to Fix It 21
   CAFFEINE 22
      Why It's a Problem 22
      How to Fix It 23
   DOING IT ALL YOURSELF 23
      Why It's a Problem 24
      How to Fix It 24
   TRYING TO MULTITASK 26
      Why It's a Problem 26
      How to Fix It 27
   NEGLECTING YOUR HEALTH 28
      Why It's a Problem 28

- *How to Fix It*.. 29
- TRYING TO DO WHAT WORKS FOR OTHERS 30
  - *Why It's a Problem* 30
  - *How to Fix It* 31
- THE WORK IS TOO HARD OR TOO EASY 32
  - *Why It's a Problem* 32
  - *How to Fix It* 33
- REACTING AND NOT PLANNING 34
  - *Why It's a Problem* 35
  - *How to Fix It* 35
- LACK OF BALANCE 36
  - *Why It's a Problem* 37
  - *How to Fix It* 38

CHAPTER 3: DOPAMINE DETOX 39

- WHAT IS DOPAMINE? 40
- WHY YOU SHOULD DOPAMINE DETOX 41
- HOW TO DETOX 43
- TRICKING YOUR BRAIN INTO DOING HARD THINGS 47
  - *Reward Yourself* 47
  - *Listen to Music* 48
  - *Weighing up the Opportunity Cost* 49

CHAPTER 4: ROUTINES FOR PRODUCTIVITY 51

- MORNINGS MATTER 52
  - *Waking Up* 52
  - *Eliminate Decision Making* 53
  - *Move a Little* 54
  - *Get Your Mind in the Zone* 55
  - *Do the Hard Thing* 56
- THE AFTERNOON SLUMP 57
  - *Eat the Right Lunch* 58
  - *Actually Take Your Break* 58
  - *Do the Easier Tasks* 59
- PRODUCTIVE EVENINGS 60
  - *Do Something You Enjoy* 61
  - *Plan for Tomorrow* 61
  - *Get Ready for Bed* 62

CHAPTER 5: MANAGING YOUR ENERGY AND ATTENTION 65

- Managing Your Energy 66
  - The Four Kinds of Energy 66
  - Increasing Your Energy Levels 69
  - Renewing Your Energy Throughout the Day 76
- Managing Your Attention 79
  - The Two Types of Attention 81
  - Focused Attention 83
  - How to Manage Attention Effectively 85

CHAPTER 6: HACK YOUR PRODUCTIVITY 87

- Set One Goal for the Day 87
- The Pomodoro Technique 88
- Regular Breaks 89
- Create a Workspace 90
- Task Management Tools 90
- Share Your Goals and Work as a Team 91
- Schedule Your Meetings Effectively 92
- Don't Have Meetings for the Sake of It 93
- When You Are Done, Switch Off 94
- Read Emails Once 95
- Write Down Things That Pop Into Your Mind 96
- Prep the Night Before 97
- Don't Lay in Bed After Your Alarm Rings 98
- Do a Quick Workout First Thing in the Morning 99
- Have Your Snacks Ready 99
- Drink Your Water 100

CHAPTER 7: BURNOUT 101

- What is Burnout? 101
- Preventing Burnout 102
  - Know Your Limits 103
  - Learn to Say No 103
  - Schedule Time to Do Nothing 104
  - Make Sure You Are Having Fun and Resting 104
  - Listen to the People Around You 105
- Resolving Burnout 106

Take a Break *106*
Focus on Your Health *107*
Reframe Your Work and Priorities *107*

CHAPTER 8: BUILDING HABITS THAT LAST **111**

STEPS TO BUILDING LONG-TERM HABITS 112
Decide What Habits You Want to Build *112*
Break Your Bad Habits *113*
Start Small and Build From There *115*
Be Consistent *116*
The Two-Day Rule *117*
A FEW HELPFUL TIPS 118
Start With One Habit *119*
Find a Role Model *119*
Know Your Why *120*

CONCLUSION **121**

REFERENCES **123**

Introduction

It seems like there is a constant drive towards being more productive. Companies develop strategies to improve employee productivity. Incentives are introduced to motivate employees to do more. And why wouldn't they? The more output the company makes the more money they will be getting. This benefits everyone in the organization. Recently, it is not just companies that are striving to be more productive—individuals are looking for ways to do it too. Because you picked up this book, I'm sure you are one of those individuals.

Have you ever asked yourself why everyone is trying to be more productive? Most people just *want* to be more productive but are unsure of the real motivator. The real motivator for increased productivity is to get more done in a specific amount of time. The ultimate reason we want to do this is to succeed at what we do and then to have spare time to pursue other things. No matter how much you love your job, you do not want to be stuck there the whole day. The less late nights you can put in without giving up quality of work, the better. This is what we all hope to achieve.

Imagine having more time to pursue the things that you want to do. Imagine having more time with your family. Imagine coming home from work and not being completely exhausted. I'm sure that is something everyone would love. We all have a specific number of hours in a day and we want to use it to the best of our ability. We want to be able to enjoy our lives as well as reach our goals. The good news is that it can be achieved if you have the right tools to do it.

This book was written because I struggled to find balance and I struggled to really perform at my best. I found that no matter how much time I put in, I was just not getting the results I wanted. It took a lot of trial and error but I finally figured out that my productivity was not only tied to the time that I put in, but it was tied to certain systems that needed to be put in place in my life. I had to learn the hard way that the more effort you put in does not necessarily lead to the best results. It is actually the right amount of effort done in the right way that gives you the results that you want. That is exactly what you will learn how to do.

This book is not about showing you how to work the bare minimum and still reach your goals. There is still work for you to do. There are still things needed from your side. The goal here is to help you to stop working extra hard for no extra reward. It is designed to help you figure out the patterns in your life that are holding you back from being as productive as you can be. If you are willing to take in the information and apply it when necessary, I have no doubt that you will be well on your way to reaching the goals you have for yourself, both in your work and in your personal life. If you are ready to get going, let's dive into Chapter 1.

Chapter 1:

The Premise of Productivity

When someone says, "wow, I've had such a productive day," they do so with a smile on their face and pride in their voice. That's all well and good but if you were to ask them why they were so productive or if they will be able to do the same the next day, there is a very slim chance they will be able to give you that information. Simply accepting that some days are more productive than others is not the right way of looking at productivity. In fact, productivity is something you can control and can improve on.

Productivity should not be a once in a while thing. It should be consistent, but in order to be consistent we have to understand what it is. If we don't actually understand productivity, we will never be able to duplicate it in our everyday lives. It will always just be something that happens on a "good day." Instead of just waiting for that good day, we should be able to make every day that good day and fulfill what we intend to. So, let's take the first step in truly understanding productivity.

The Definition of Productivity

Depending on who you ask, their definition of productivity will differ. Some people say it is getting things done according to a deadline. Others will say it is accomplishing the most amount of tasks in a limited time frame. Some simply won't even know what productivity is at all.

The root word of productive is produce. This means that in order to be productive, you have to be producing something. You have to be doing something that is yielding a product or a result. Companies also measure productivity. Their standards are a little bit different from personal productivity, since they focus on the total workforce output, so they will look at the amount of their product being produced. With personal productivity, it is not all about putting out something. Think about studying; you could have had a productive day studying but you don't have anything physical to show for it.

If you are looking for a quick one-line definition of productivity, it would be this: The relevant output of a person in a certain amount of time that moves them closer to their goal.

Measuring Productivity

It is safe to say that productivity will not look the same for everyone. Every person has different goals, life situations, and time slots in which to be productive. However, that does not mean that you cannot measure your productivity. In fact, measuring your productivity is one of the best things you can do. It will keep you motivated and highlight exactly what you need to get done.

If we don't measure or track our productivity then we will never truly know whether we have actually been productive or not. Let's be honest here, how many times have you gotten through a busy day only to realize that you are nowhere as close to reaching your goal as you thought you were? This has happened to the best of us. We have all fallen into the trap of believing that if we are busy then that must mean that we are being productive. This mindset actually tires us out before we can even get close to accomplishing what we want to.

Remember the definition for productivity given in the previous section? It said the *relevant* output of a person in a certain amount of time that moves them closer to their goal, the key word here being *relevant*. Doing things that are not relevant to meeting your goals cannot be counted as productivity, that is simply just busywork.

When you are trying to measure your productivity, you can only measure the relevant work. This is the work that actually matters; the work that will get you closer to your desired result. For example, if you are a writer, you should measure the number of words you have written or if you are a teacher, you could measure the number of tests you have marked. Simply measuring the amount of time you sat at your desk will not work for measuring how productive you have been for the day. The only way you will be able to measure how productive you have been is to set the right objectives and then see how close you have come to meeting them. This way you will know if you have actually gotten closer to meeting your end goal.

Setting Measurable Objectives

Now that we know that the only way to measure productivity is to set objectives, the next question you should be asking is, "how do I set measurable objectives?"

Great question! I'm about to show you exactly how to do that.

First things first, you need to know what the end goal is. Knowing what you are working towards will help you create the next steps and keep you motivated as you go along. Look at it this way, if you went on a walk but had no destination in mind, there would be a point where you would stop, turn back, and go home. This is because there is no good reason for you to continue. But, if you knew you were going to go to your friends house or that your goal is walking three miles, then you would keep going until you reached that goal. You would keep pushing even if it started getting hard or if you just didn't feel like it anymore. There is something that you are trying to reach.

This is the same with our daily activity. Just sitting at our desks and doing whatever task pops up first is an incredibly ineffective way to go about your tasks. It puts you at the mercy of whatever catches your attention first, and that might not be what is most important or the thing that will yield results. Your end goal does not always have to be a big project, it can be something small, like getting through 50 emails in the day. The important thing is that you know what your goal is right from the start.

Alright, so let's look at how to set measurable objectives with the end goal in mind. Let's pretend that you are going to build a model rocket. Below are three lists of objectives that will eventually lead you to the end goal. Can you spot the most effective one?

List A

1. buy all the needed supplies
2. build the model rocket
3. launch

List B

1. research how to build a model rocket
2. make a list of supplies needed and purchase them
3. prepare and build the engine mount
4. prepare and build fins

5. make the body of the rocket and mark out where the other pieces should fit
6. attach engine mount and fins to the body
7. attach launch lug and shock cord
8. attach parachute
9. attach the nose to the rocket
10. paint and decorate
11. launch

List C

1. research how to build a model rocket
2. make a list of supplies needed
3. see what you already have in your house
4. find out where to buy them
5. buy the wood
6. buy the plastic pieces
7. buy the glue
8. buy the tools
9. buy the tubing
10. buy the parachute
11. buy the cords and other extras
12. cut out the engine mount
13. glue pieces together
14. draw fins on the wood
15. cut out fins
16. sand any rough edges on the fins
17. (okay, I think you get the point so I'm going to stop this list right here) bonus tip: this is definitely not the correct list

The correct answer is List B. This is a list of objectives—as you complete them you can easily see that you are getting closer to the goal. It is not too long or too short. It offers guidance but is in no way overwhelming. You will probably be able to tick one or two things off the list during each work session.

List A is way too short. If you were to create a list of objectives like this, how long do you suppose it would take to tick something off it? It would probably be a few days at least. This does not allow you to see your progress. Even though you are doing the work, there is no way for you to measure how productive you have been in each work session. You have a clear end goal but no measurable steps towards that goal. This is often why people get demotivated halfway through projects and large tasks.

List C is unnecessarily long. This is a common mistake people make when creating a list of tasks or objectives. For one, if I had carried on until the end, this list could have easily had 30 things on it. Just looking at it is demotivating. Nobody wants to look at a to-do list that is so long it feels like it can't be completed in a reasonable amount of time. Steps 1 to 11 in list C are all encompassed in steps 1 and 2 in list B. Overcomplicating your objectives will end up demotivating you and make the task look way bigger than it is. You will also end up spending so much time looking at the list, trying to tick stuff off that you will be wasting the time you could actually be using to be productive.

You now understand how to set objectives in a way that will allow you to measure your productivity. This is essential if you want to know how productive you have been throughout the day or the week. As we go through the rest of this book, we are going to go through many different ways in which you can increase your productivity. It would be a great exercise for you to take some time and write down what you think your most productive day would look like. Place time stamps and write it out like a schedule, as you would if you were planning out your day on a normal weekday. As you continue to read through the chapters of this book, keep coming back to it and see if there is anything that you can change that would make your day more productive. When you are done with the book, you should have a guideline of what you need to change or improve on in your everyday life.

Chapter 2:

What Prevents Productivity

There are plenty of things that prevent you from being as productive as you should be. Some are quite obvious and others are things that you would never think about. It will be beneficial to go through this list and find the ones that are applicable to you. Some are more prominent in your life than others. Once you are aware of the things that block you from being productive, you can implement the correct solutions.

Procrastination

This is easily one of the most well-known reasons for someone not being productive. Procrastination is the act of putting something off until later. There are many reasons we do this, including overestimating the time we have to complete the task or that we simply just don't feel like doing it. Procrastinators aren't necessarily lazy, as they will fill the time doing something else so that they don't have to do the task they are avoiding. This means that procrastination is an avoidance technique and not just "not wanting to work." It is often specifically related to the task that needs to be done. So, instead of working on that proposal for work, you start doing the dishes and cleaning the house. This leads to wasting time with unimportant things instead of getting the things done that need to get done.

Why It's a Problem

It is clear to see why procrastination is a problem. Simply put, you will not get anything done efficiently if you procrastinate. Sure, you will be filling your time with something, but that thing will probably not be giving you the output that you need.

Procrastination happens to the best of us. Almost every person has struggled with it at some point in their life. The reason is that hard work is hardly ever attractive but there are many other things that are more fun or just easier to do. If you have ever needed to study for an exam, you may have found yourself cleaning your room, organizing your desk, or labeling your stationary instead of actually studying. None of these tasks are bad, in fact, you should probably do them at some point, but they will probably not help you pass the exam. However, they are easier than actually studying, so you find yourself doing these tasks and it feels like you are being productive when you are actually wasting time.

The thing about procrastination is that it does not take the undesirable task away, it just gives you less time to do it in the future. You will probably not be able to give the task your best because you will just be focused on trying to finish it on time. Most of the all-nighters students have had to pull was due to them procrastinating and not because they actually did not have enough time. Students are not the only ones who struggle with this, admin staff, lawyers, corporate employees, and stay at home parents all struggle with procrastination. In fact, anyone who has to do a less than enjoyable task is at risk of procrastination.

How to Fix It

The only way you will be able to stop procrastinating is to get serious about doing the task. Plan your day out and limit distractions. If you know that you will more than likely want to clean your room as a distraction from studying, plan to do this in advance so that when you sit down to study, you won't have that excuse. Even better, study somewhere else—like a library.

You have to recognize that you are a procrastinator for you to plan to beat it. Chances are, you already know if you struggle with procrastination. If not, all you have to do is think back on your last few deadlines or projects. Were you rushing to get it done at the last minute even though you knew about it well before the due date? If you answered yes then you, my friend, are a procrastinator.

There are a few things you can do to help break the habit of procrastination. You can do them all together or just pick one or two to try. Chances are that after you have implemented one of these strategies for a while, it will stop being effective. Once it stops working, change to another strategy. You can also yoyo between them. Find what works for you and do that. Here are the procrastination cures:

- Change your environment - try working outside, at a coffee shop, or just change up something about your work space.
- Break down your work - splitting up your work into smaller tasks will help it seem manageable. You will find that you will be more motivated to do smaller chunks of work.
- Identify your distractions - chances are that you are being distracted by the same things over and over. Find out what those are and remove them. If it's a certain app, delete it from your phone. If you procrastinate by cooking elaborate meals at lunchtime, prep your meals in advance.
- Be accountable - Tell someone about the goals you have for the day and have them check up on you to see if you have done them. We are always more motivated to do something if someone else knows about it because we don't want to let them down.

Cellphones and Notifications

In today's technology driven world, this is becoming a bigger problem than ever. Phones and apps add so much to our lives but they can also be a massive distraction. If we don't put the right boundaries in place, we will find ourselves scrolling for hours or playing our favorite game instead of doing what we need to do.

Why It's a Problem

There are many studies, articles, and documentaries out there that highlight why we are so addicted to that little metal box we slip into our pockets. It's not the actual phone that is the problem but our addiction to not missing out, especially since it's so easy to be connected to everything going on in the span of a second. This is what makes us want to check our phones every few minutes even when we don't have any notifications.

Notifications are a problem on their own. Once we hear the notification, we have to check what is going on, otherwise we feel like we are missing out on something important. Even if we don't check our phones after hearing the notification, we are now distracted and our minds are off the task at hand. This means that we have to use extra willpower and energy to get back on track.

How to Fix It

The solutions to this are pretty simple, but actually doing them can prove to be quite challenging. The first step is to put your phone away or put it on silent. Many people struggle with this because they want to be accessible in an emergency, but if we are really honest with ourselves, how many emergencies happen in a day that we absolutely have to be available immediately? What about in the week? Or even a month? Probably not any. Most things can wait for a few hours but we have conditioned ourselves to believe that there might be something urgent that will happen so we need our phones. I promise the world won't burn down if you put it away for a few hours.

If you absolutely must have your phone with you, then silence all notifications. Notify your close friends and family that if they need to get a hold of you urgently, they must call. This will allow you to still be available in an emergency and lessen the distractions.

The problem with having your phone close to you is that you will be tempted to check it. Once you switch on the phone you will want to log onto your favorite app or check social media, and then suddenly you have wasted an hour of your day. To prevent this from happening, download an app that blocks all other apps (I know, another app—ironic isn't it?). App blockers will do just as the name says. If you click on an app, it won't let you go on. This creates some resistance, so you just end up closing it and getting back to what you were doing. A big part of why we get distracted by our phones is that it is so easy to log on and before you can even think about it, you are caught up in the app. The app blockers stop you and give you time to think about what you are doing.

Another thing you could try is to turn your phone's grayscale mode on. The colors on your screen make it so much more attractive to look at. If everything is greyed out, you will actually end up spending less time on your phone. Think about it, how boring does a feed of grey Instagram pictures look? It is far less addicting.

The place we get stuck with our phones the most is in our beds. Either we can't put it down at night and end up sleeping so late that we are dead tired in the morning, or we pick the phone up first thing when we wake up and waste the whole morning. Many people actually do both. Starting and ending your day on your phone is just not a good idea. Rather, make your bedroom a no phone zone. Place your phone on a table outside your bedroom—you will still be able to hear it if someone calls. Purchase an alarm clock if you are scared that you won't wake up in time. There is really no good reason for your phone to follow you into bed.

Emails

Everyone from the corporate office worker to the freelancer uses email. It is a great tool to notify and communicate with the people you work with. However, it can be a huge distraction from the work that you need to be doing.

Why It's a Problem

Often people don't think of email as the enemy of productivity, but if you look at your day and see how much of your time is spent reading and answering emails, you will probably be shocked. We can so easily spend half of the work day looking at and replying to emails. That means we only have half the time to do the work we are getting paid to do.

Emails are distracting because we have to answer them immediately. When an email comes in, we stop what we are doing to answer it. The truth is that we don't even have to answer most of the emails we get immediately. Hardly anyone ever expects to get an immediate reply to an email. If it really was an urgent thing, then they would give you a call to make sure you got the message.

If you see an email about a task you have to do later or the next day, your mind already starts planning. So even though you don't have to do anything for it right now, your brain is no longer concentrating on the task you were doing before the email came in. This is the biggest problem with always checking emails. If there are no boundaries when it comes to your email, your day will quickly be overtaken by it.

How to Fix It

The only way to fix this problem is to stop checking your emails throughout the day. Which is, again, easier said than done. It is just like the phone notifications, as soon as you see an email come in you want to check it. This means that you need to stop the notification from coming through. You can easily do that in your email settings. Remember to do this for both your phone and computer.

I'm not saying that you should never check your emails. Emails are important but they need to be prioritized correctly. The best thing you can do is to set aside a specific time to go through them. If you work for yourself, you can send a notice out to your clients and customers saying that you will be replying to your emails after a certain time. This is usually not necessary because like I said earlier, most people don't expect an immediate response to emails.

If you are setting aside an hour or two to just focus on emails, make sure it is not in your most productive time. Emails don't really require much brain power, so they can be done with little effort. Replying to emails when you know you will be a little tired is completely fine. Use the time when you are most alert and energetic to do your most important tasks.

If your job is quite email-intensive then you will probably have to set up a few times during the day to reply to them. Try creating two or three slots in your day dedicated to answering emails. This way you will be able to reply promptly but you have blocked out time to do the other important tasks you need to get done.

Some companies have worked on email systems that help their employees to be more productive. They use color coding or acronyms in the subject line to indicate how urgent the email is. For instance:

- Blue - not urgent, just informative and does not need a response. Employees can get to it whenever it suits them.

- Yellow - needs action or acknowledgement, not particularly urgent but should be checked sometime during the day or week.
- Red - very urgent, needs action ASAP.

This is a very basic example so you can customize it to your needs. If you are an employee, you can try approaching your manager with this suggestion. If you are a manager or owner of a company, then you should consider putting an effective structure to deal with emails. Your employees will thank you and you will see an increase in company productivity.

Clutter

When we are in a rush to get things done or working towards strict deadlines, the last thing on our minds is cleaning up. If you walk into the office of someone who is working on a big project, it is common to see the space at least a little bit cluttered. While doing a full spring clean of your work space may not be the best idea when you have a deadline; working in a neat area definitely does help with productivity.

Why It's a Problem

Clutter creates a barrier for productivity because it opens the door for distractions. When we see things that are out of place or that spark a thought in a direction that is not the task at hand, our minds start to wander. The clutter is basically competing for our attention. The clutter does not have to be a hot mess of papers, files, or other random items; it could just be a few small things that are not related to the task at hand like a photo of your family or even an ornament.

If you are constantly being distracted by the things around you it will make doing your job really difficult. When we are doing something that is not really pleasant, our minds automatically want to run away and find something easier or more fun to do. Having lots of different items around that could remind you of other tasks, spark a thought in your mind, or just makes you want to clean up your space will end up making you unproductive.

How to Fix It

Everybody's definition of clutter is different. Some people prefer to work in a spotless workstation where nothing is out of place, but other people might find that boring and it kills their creativity. So, when trying to declutter your space you have to be conscious of what kind of person you are and how much tolerance you have for clutter.

As a general rule you should not have anything in your line of sight that is not related to the task. If it is something that inspires you or you need it to complete your task, like an award or motivating quote, then it is fine to have it there. It will serve as a reminder to get back to your task if your mind ever does wander.

Try and do a clean-up every week. Don't leave it for when you are supposed to be working, this is just asking for distraction. Set a day and time to declutter your space. Put it in your calendar and make sure you only do it for the allocated time. Making it a part of your tasks will also help you feel like you are doing something to get closer to reaching your goals.

Caffeine

Many people can't start their day without a cup of coffee. There is definitely nothing wrong with having a few cups when needed; the problem comes when you are completely dependent on it.

Why It's a Problem

In the short term, caffeine does increase alertness and energy but as the day drags on, the effects wear off. This is why you keep reaching for that cup of coffee or that energy drink. It is also why it is easy to overdo it with the caffeine. Too much caffeine can cause dehydration, jitters, headaches, and even brain fog.

The other problem with caffeine is that it is highly addictive. Coffee people often need to have at least four or five cups of coffee a day to feel satisfied. If they dont get their caffeine fix it impacts their energy levels and they will also start getting headaches. Their bodies are too dependent on it. It is never good to be dependent on something else for energy.

How to Fix It

This one is pretty simple. All you have to do is limit your caffeine intake. This is definitely easier said than done, especially if you are someone who is very dependent on caffeine already. A slow weaning process is the best approach. Going cold-turkey will probably cause some withdrawal symptoms.

If you choose to completely cut out caffeine, then do it at a time when you don't have a packed schedule. This way, if you do have withdrawal symptoms you won't have a heavy workload on top of that. Otherwise, slowly lowering your caffeine intake every week is a good way to go. You can have one cup of coffee or energy drink less than you normally do and keep decreasing your intake weekly.

Doing It All Yourself

I know this book is about you becoming more productive but that does not mean that you have to do everything yourself. We often struggle to ask for help because we fear looking incompetent or being a nuisance. This holds us back in the long run.

Why It's a Problem

If the person in the office next door had the instruction manual that had all the answers to the project you were working on, wouldn't you want it? The answer is probably yes. Anyone would be able to tell you that getting that instruction manual is more efficient than trying to complete the project by yourself. You would probably cut out hours of frustration and use that energy to actually make progress on the project.

This makes sense to anyone reading this, but it is not what most of us do. We always want to figure things out ourselves, even when there is someone else who has done it already and has the information to help us. All we have to do is ask the people with the knowledge we need to help us with the task. There are very few situations in which people would refuse to share their knowledge or guide us in the right direction.

Now, I'm not advocating for being lazy. You definitely don't want to be labeled as the person that cannot do anything for themselves. You should always try something first. See if you can figure it out on your own, but know your limits. Know when you are not getting anywhere and it's time to seek help. If you have tried about two or three times and still can't figure it out, then it is probably safe to go and ask for help.

How to Fix It

Of course, the only way to fix this is to go and ask for help when you are stuck. When you do this, remember that the way you ask matters. People don't want to help someone if they feel like they are being taken advantage of or if they think that you are just too lazy to figure it out yourself. This is why it is important to know when and how to ask.

When you approach someone to ask for help or guidance, you need to do it in a way that will make them feel like the bigger person. This is especially helpful to keep in mind when you are dealing with a difficult person. Starting off your petition with a compliment is a good idea. Think about the reason you are asking them for help and not anyone else. Are they particularly good at this type of thing? Have you noticed them do it before? Do you know they have the skill set for what you need help with? Once you know why you are asking them you can fashion your question around that.

Showing them that you tried to complete the task yourself is also really important. Like I said earlier, nobody wants to help a lazy person. Showing them that you did try and then showing them how you failed will prove to them that you are actually willing to do the work and not just looking for the easy way out. When asking for help from someone above you, like a boss or manager, this is an even more important step. It shows that you are proactive and want to grow and learn.

Trying to Multitask

I'm sure we all have heard someone bragging about being a great multitasker. It seems like the more we are able to do at a time the more productive we can be. The only problem is that we can't do more than one thing effectively. This is especially true when it comes to more difficult tasks.

Why It's a Problem

There are some things that we can multitask at. When you are ironing, you can still listen to a podcast and do the job quite well. The problem is that we will definitely miss out on some points in the podcast. Ironing is a pretty mundane task and it requires very little brain power, but there are some points that require a little more concentration. In those moments when you are trying to decide what the best way to iron that specific fabric is, or whatever slight challenge that may come up, you cannot fully focus on what is being said in the podcast.

In reality, we cannot multitask and be 100% effective in either task we are doing. One will take our attention and we will leave the other behind. Now I'm not saying that you shouldn't watch TV or listen to podcasts when you are doing mundane tasks like cleaning or folding laundry, but you definitely should not try and multitask when doing something important. The reason being that it is very difficult to mess up on folding clothes and even if you do, it's an easy fix. If you mess up on a spreadsheet or report for work, the repercussions will be much more serious.

How to Fix It

The best way to go about completing your tasks is to focus on each one individually and block out time to do them. Even saying you will work on this task for one hour, then move to the next, and then come back to the first one is just not effective. Some people think about it as having variety in their work day but it is very difficult to be efficient like that.

If you have very big tasks to get done, try working on each one for the longest time possible. This does not mean not taking breaks, but just allowing you mind to only think about one thing at a time. So if you have two tasks to get done over the weekend; work on one on Saturday and do the other on Sunday. This way, you only have one thing to think about on each day and your brain does not have to keep switching between tasks.

For all the students out there that think you can catch up on your favorite show and study, you cannot! You might think that you are studying or making notes but whatever information that is in front of you is not actually going into your head. You are going to have to go over it again for it to stick. This means that you are taking twice as long to study or make notes. It is far better to study for a while and when you feel like you need a break, watch your show. You will actually finish studying much quicker and get to enjoy your show properly.

Neglecting Your Health

The most important thing in our lives should be our health. If we are not healthy we can never perform at our best. We will always fall short because we cannot physically do any more. So many people neglect their health for the sake of convenience. We see a rise in obesity, heart disease, and diabetes all over the world. People live more sedentary lives because it is easier to do so.

Health is not only about what we are eating. Sleep, mental health, and exercise all play a part. We need to make sure we have balance in all these areas for us to be truly healthy. If we don't take care of one of these categories it will affect the others. The less healthy we are, the less productive we will be.

Why It's a Problem

We need a clear mind and a healthy body in order for us to perform tasks in the most productive manner. If we are not healthy we will get tired more quickly, we will have to take more frequent breaks, and we will not be able to concentrate properly. When this happens we reach for a quick fix, which is usually caffeine, and we already know why caffeine is not great for us.

When we are not healthy mentally, we can suffer from brain fog, are easily stressed, and can get overwhelmed quickly. If not dealt with then this can cripple us. We need to have a healthy body and a healthy mind for us to work at our best.

How to Fix It

The only way to fix this problem is to fight it at the root. You will have to assess yourself and find out what part of your life is unhealthy. Do you not get enough nutrients in your diet? Are your friends toxic? Are you exercising? Do you drink too much alcohol or abuse other substances? Are you not sleeping enough?

Take some time to do some introspection. Find out the parts of your life that are not healthy and that are putting strain on your mind and body. If you need some help with this, ask your friends and family. They can usually see unhealthy patterns before you do. They will also be able to help you develop a plan to improve the unhealthy part of your life.

If you don't do any exercise during the week then perhaps start by taking a walk every evening after dinner. This can do wonders for both your physical health and your mental health. If you are eating takeout almost every day, start making nutritious home-cooked meals.

Exercise and eating right will also help improve your sleep. If you are tired you will never perform as efficiently as you could be. A well-rested you will be able to complete tasks in about half the time of a sleep-deprived you. Plan your days by prioritizing getting seven to eight hours of rest per night and you will see how much better you are able to function the next day. You will also notice that you will be able to eat better because you won't be craving sugar for an energy fix. You will also have more energy to exercise. A good night's rest is one of the best and easiest things you can do for your health.

Trying to Do What Works for Others

I'm sure your parents have given you the "everyone is unique" speech. As we get older, we forget that we are each different and have slightly different needs. So instead of focusing on ourselves, we see what others are doing and immediately try and implement it in our lives. When it doesn't work we get frustrated. We need to be doing things the way that will work for us, not because it works for others.

Why It's a Problem

Since everyone is different, certain things will work better for others than for you. There's nothing wrong with trying out new methods of doing things or trying out different work styles or environments, but don't think that just because it worked for others it will work for you.

Often, we get stuck in the mentality that copying someone else's work style will be beneficial to us. Then we try to force ourselves to do it that way. The longer we spend trying to fit ourselves into a specific way of doing something, the more time we are wasting.

Some people prefer waking up at 5am to start work while others are night owls. Some prefer listening to music while working while others work better in complete silence. Some like an office environment and others work better outdoors in the fresh air. Once you have found out what you like and what works best for you, there is no need to conform to the way everyone else wants to do something.

How to Fix It

The only way to remedy this is to figure out what works for you. If you don't know what your preferred work environment is, then try a few and see what is best for you. Find out what makes you concentrate more and what inspires you. Try working outside, listening to music while you work, or taking frequent breaks. Once you have this sorted, you don't need to force yourself to work like other people do. Of course, feel free to try new things but as soon as you see it's not working then go back to what does.

If you find that your preferred working environment or style is not being catered to by your current job, it might be worth it to approach your boss with this. All you have to do is say you noticed that this specific thing helps you to be more productive and ask if you would be able to include it to your work routine. There is no harm in asking, unless what you are requesting is completely outrageous or expensive for the company.

The Work Is Too Hard or Too Easy

Humans are meant to take on challenges and to solve problems. Just think about the times when you figured something out, built something, or presented something you were really proud of. Things that are challenging and we are able to figure out pushes us to be better, learn more, and motivates us for the future.

However, there is another side to this. If the work is too hard it may end up demotivating us. Doing work that is either too hard or too easy can have a massive impact on our productivity. Challenge is definitely needed but there is such a thing as too much and while we might think that we like things to be easy, it can have the same effect as work that is too hard.

Why It's a Problem

Let's first talk about work that is too hard. We all have a certain skill level and ability. As much as we want to believe that anything is possible if we put our minds to it, this isn't necessarily true. If you were to give a second grader an algebra sum they would be very confused and would not be able to do it. This does not mean that they are not smart, but they simply just don't have the right knowledge and skill set to complete the task. They will eventually gain the knowledge that they need but that will take quite a few years. It's the same for us as adults. We can always gain skills and knowledge but sometimes we just don't have what we need to complete the task.

Trying to do something that is above our skill level can demotivate us and kill our productivity. We can only work on something for so long without making progress on it before we get frustrated with it. We can easily feel as though we are the problem and that will transfer into every other area of our lives.

On the other hand, tasks that are too easy just get mundane if done for too long. Performing tasks that don't challenge us at all does not allow us to be creative and use our brains the way it was meant to be used. Eventually, we start doing things just for the sake of it and as soon as something more interesting pops up, we run to it. This ends in us taking much longer to do the easier tasks than what is actually needed. Of course, there will always be mundane tasks to do in everyday life, but our entire day or job function should not equal this.

How to Fix It

This can be an incredibly difficult one to fix, especially in a corporate context. If you are working for someone else, it can be difficult to have control over the difficulty of the projects you get. The best thing you can do is speak to your manager about the problems you have been having. If the work is too difficult, perhaps you can ask to do a course to increase your skill level. If the work is too easy, ask for something more challenging or maybe try and find a new job where your needs will be met.

If you work for yourself or are seeking productivity in a more personal context, it can be easier to change the types of tasks you are doing. Try and find ways to challenge yourself or gain new skills to make tasks easier. It also helps to ask other people for help if the task you are busy with seems too difficult for you.

If one aspect of your life is much too easy, try and challenge yourself in another aspect. The goal is to challenge your brain in some area. You could pick up a new project, start studying, or develop a side hustle. Fixing the "too-easy problem" is easier than trying to work around tasks that are too difficult for you. Sometimes the only solution for this is to ask for that task to be removed from your plate until you have developed the skills necessary to complete it.

Reacting and Not Planning

This is a very common problem and not many people can actually pick it up. We often get to work and have a rough idea of what needs to be done, but as soon as someone asks us to do something we drop the current task for the new one. This is reacting to the situation instead of taking it and adding it to the plan for the day.

If we are always reacting to emails and requests it is very difficult to be productive in our daily lives.

Why It's a Problem

We are always more productive when we plan things through. Knowing what we need to get done and how long it will take helps us to plan our day effectively. As soon as we pick up tasks that are not on the original plan, we have to give up something to fit in the new task. This is how we end up missing deadlines or getting overwhelmed with the amount of work we have at the end of the day.

How to Fix It

Throughout the workday people will always be coming in and asking things of you. This is especially so if you work in an office environment. Just because someone makes a request does not mean that you have to do it right now, or at all. Prioritizing your tasks will help you figure out what is important and what is not.

The first thing you are going to have to do is write down everything you need to get done for the day. The most important things should be done first since you have more energy for them and there is less of a chance for interruptions. If something does pop up, you need to ask yourself how important it is in relation to what you are doing. If it is less important then leave it until you are done with what you are currently doing. It also helps to not check emails or take phone calls when you are busy with something important. If that is an option then it is one of the most effective things you can do for your productivity.

Ask the people around you to send you an email when they need something rather than walking into your office and distracting you. You can then have a dedicated time to go through your emails and see if there is anything important that you need to get done for the day. You could go through your mail at about midday to see if you need to restructure your day with any new tasks that have been given to you.

It is so important to never just drop what you are doing for another task. This creates confusion in your schedule and results in you not knowing what you are doing. It is very easy to lose track of where you were if you have to leave it for later. If there really is an emergency or urgent task that needs to get done, then there isn't much you can do about it so you will have to drop what you are doing. But this is definitely not the norm. You would be surprised at how many tasks are not as urgent as you think they are when you take a step back to prioritize them.

Lack of Balance

I'm sure you have heard of people trying to live a balanced life. Everyone is striving for this balance, but what exactly is it? Balance is taking all areas of your life into consideration and making sure that each is getting the attention it deserves. It is very easy to get off balance if we are not actively striving for it. If we only focus on one area of our lives, the others will suffer. This can cause major problems because we need all areas of our lives to be taken care of in order for us to be healthy and happy.

Why It's a Problem

Everything about us is interconnected. It's difficult to try and be the best we can be but leave out one area of our lives. Often, we are only thinking about being productive with our work tasks and then we let the other areas of our lives suffer. Our rest time, relationships, mental health, fitness, nutrition, and sleep are all areas that need to be given attention.

Once one of these areas is lacking, we can get demotivated, unhappy, or sluggish. The automatic response is to put more effort into our work but that will have adverse effects. All you have to do is look at the source of the breakdowns of many famous business people and entrepreneurs. Divorces, mental breakdowns, loss of friends, and strife within family are very commonplace in people who spend all their time working and don't put in the effort into the other areas of their lives. You will see that their breakdowns were not caused by not putting enough effort into their work, but rather neglecting the other areas of their lives.

How to Fix It

If you are going through a slump or you feel as though something in your life is not right, the best thing you can do is figure out what is lacking. Take some time to step back from work or whatever is taking up most of your time. Think about all the other important things in your life and be honest about what is being neglected. Once you have figured out what area you have neglected, you can work on fixing it.

Finding a balance should not only be done when you notice that you are completely off balance. Rather, make a plan so that you never get to that stage. Decide how much time and energy each area of your life needs. Then schedule time for each area. Some of these don't need blocks of time, but need a change in habits. Find ways to eat healthier, move your body more, and do things you enjoy.

Chapter 3:

Dopamine Detox

You have probably heard about dopamine detoxing or dopamine fasting by now. It has taken the world by storm as a way to reset the brain to enjoy the simpler things in life and to find pleasure in things that we no longer do. While there is no such thing as resetting the brain or removing dopamine from the equation completely, there are some definite benefits to a dopamine detox.

In today's world we are overstimulated. We are all on the hunt for the next pleasurable experience and things that give us that hit of dopamine are very easily available to us. This means we no longer desire to do things that don't make us feel good, even if those things are most beneficial for us in the long run. We'd rather do the things that offer instant gratification. This is becoming a massive problem, not only in the workplace, but also in everyday life. This is the reason it is so important to change some of the patterns in our lives.

What Is Dopamine?

First things first, let's actually discuss what dopamine is. For many years, people have thought dopamine was simply a pleasure chemical. It would be triggered by something we like and then we would have a rush of dopamine, which would make us want to do that thing again. So instead of being responsible for us feeling pleasure, it is responsible for us anticipating that we will get something pleasurable by engaging with someone or performing an action.

Dopamine is actually more related to motivation and is part of a larger reward system in our brain (Akers, 2019). In this system, dopamine is released when your body is expecting a reward, and this is what motivates us to do things. Naturally, we are more inclined to do things if there is going to be a reward at the end of it. For example, when we hear the notification tone on our phones, dopamine is released. This makes us want to check the phone to see the message or notification that caused the sound. There is no guarantee that it will be something pleasurable, like a loved one sending us a message, but we will still want to check it because there is a chance that it could be something pleasurable. We want to check the phone because there is an opportunity for a pleasurable experience. This also explains why people will still gamble after losing lots of money—they do it in the hopes of getting something good. Every time they pull the lever on the slot machine they get a hit of dopamine that motivates them to keep going.

This type of association is what causes dopamine to be continuously released. If there was a stimulus that resulted in a reward, your brain will release dopamine when you come into contact with that stimulus again. If you smell chocolate chip cookies, you will want to eat chocolate chip cookies; the smell is the stimulus.

Dopamine does play a big part in this process but it is not the only function it participates in. It is also involved in blood flow, digestion, mood, emotions, stress, and sleep, among other things. This is why the premise of fasting from dopamine is not entirely correct. You can't actually make your body produce less dopamine; you can only control the triggers. Just know that throughout this chapter when you see the terms dopamine fasting or dopamine detox, it is not referring to the actual limiting of dopamine or the lessening of it in our bodies.

Why You Should Dopamine Detox

Of recent years people have become more aware of their bad habits and the things that are hindering them from moving forward. This is because there is a lot more stimuli out there that causes bad habits than there ever was before. Things are more accessible and that is both good and bad. Learning how to control ourselves and what we spend our time on is crucial if we ever want to reach our goals and reach our full potentials.

The reason for the dopamine detox is to take your focus off the things that take up your time but yield no long-term reward. We are often so stuck on things that give us instant gratification that we no longer want to do things that give us no immediate reward. That is why people rather have thousands of Instagram followers instead of putting the work in to make the relationships with their friends and family work. People would rather sit and binge-eat fast food than eat healthy and go to the gym, or would rather browse the internet than work on their business idea.

Unfortunately, the things that require more work and are harder to do are better for us in the long-run. The more we do those hard things, the more successful we will be in our lives. The temptations will always be there, we can't ask the world to stop moving forward because we are struggling to do what we are supposed to. As the world progresses, there will likely be more distractions and even more things that stimulate our want for instant gratification. It is our job to get a hold of our lives. We need to be able to have the self-control necessary and put the systems in place to be successful and productive.

In every context of life, we can't let ourselves be controlled by the things that seem fun and make us happy for a moment. This detox will help you gain a little bit more control over yourself and the things you do. It helps us to be mindful of the things around you. Getting time away from distractions will help you learn more about yourself. You will figure out what actually makes you happy and what you enjoy doing. Your relationships will be given space to flourish and your overall productivity will improve. You will be able to find happiness in little things and be able to appreciate the world around you more. Doesn't that sound so much better than being constantly distracted by things that won't offer you much in the long term?

How to Detox

You can't actually reset your dopamine levels but you can avoid the triggers, which is what this detox is about. You need to know what your triggers are so that you can put the necessary steps in place to avoid them or limit them. As much as we all think we are strong and can say no to the things that offer us this simple hit of dopamine, we are not. Having the temptations around us will make us more likely to engage with it. Even if you can say no for a little while, your power will run out eventually and you will be back to square one.

The first thing you need to do is determine what you need to detox from. Since there are many dopamine triggers, you have to see which ones are applicable to you. The most common behavioral addictions are:

- food (mostly unhealthy foods, high in sugar and fat)
- gambling or shopping
- pornography and self-pleasure
- cellphones, the internet and gaming
- thrill seeking
- drugs and alcohol

Your triggers could be quite a few things on the list, or maybe just one. If you do suffer with a drug or alcohol addiction, it is best to seek out professional help. These are in a different category than the others because they alter the chemicals in the brain and affect the body directly. In any of these categories, if you struggle with a very bad addiction then you should seek out professional help. If you try and do it by yourself you will probably experience withdrawal symptoms that will make the process very difficult for you. A professional will be able to guide you through it and advise you on what is best for you.

When dopamine detoxes are spoken about they are usually referring to digital detoxes. The thing is that there are so many other things that can affect you in a similar way that it wouldn't make sense to just talk about the digital aspect. Being aware of every area that could be a problem for you will allow you to work through all of your weak spots and become an overall better person by the end of it. I would also just like to say that the point of this is not to remove all sources of pleasure or reward from your life. That would be absolute torture, I'm sure. You are just learning to control your impulses and triggers by way of a type of detox.

Since cell phones, the internet, and gaming is one of the biggest distractions and dopamine triggers we will use it in this example. I think every single one of us can say we are addicted to these things at some level. You can replace this with any other thing on the list that you happen to be struggling with. Also, you don't have to remove all of these from your life at once. Leaving one of them should be fine but eventually the aim is to get a handle on all of these addictions.

In order for you to detox properly you have to take a drastic first step. Take your phone, computer, tablet, or whatever it is and lock it away for a whole day. I know, you are probably panicking all ready. The thing is that we do not need these devices as much as we think we do; we have developed a dependence on them and get anxious when we don't have access to them. This is a problem because these things are not fundamental to our survival, we just treat them like they are. The only thing that could get a pass is your phone if you absolutely need it for some reason. This reason cannot be to chat with your friends or to update your status. I promise the people around you will be fine without speaking to you for a day. If you do need your phone then you need to disconnect from the internet; if there is an emergency, notify the respective parties that they will need to call you to reach you.

While you are away from all forms of technology and the internet, you will need to find something else to fill your time. It might actually be very hard because usually if you are bored you can just switch on Netflix or play a game on your phone. Now that you don't have that option, you will need to find other ways of entertaining yourself. I'm not going to lie to you, you will be very bored at various parts of the day. You might even just end up sitting and daydreaming. This is good, it will show you how much you actually rely on technology and how much control it has over you. Throughout the day you will have to resist the urge to go and get your phone or switch on the TV.

You are allowed to do plenty of things. Just pretend that you are back in the olden days without technology. You can spend some intentional time with your family, cook an elaborate meal, go for a walk, volunteer somewhere, read a book, or pick up a new hobby. You might even find something you really enjoy. The thing is that everything releases some level of dopamine, even drinking an ice-cold glass of water on a hot day. We just don't appreciate it as much because we have gotten used to the higher dopamine levels of these more addictive behaviors. We have basically lost our dopamine sensitivity and the goal of these detoxes are to get it back. That is why you need to find other things that you like doing, they will release dopamine even if it is a smaller amount. Eventually, you will feel more satisfied and happier by doing these tasks.

You can do this kind of detox day as often as you would like. A good suggestion is to do it once a month. Just completely shut off. When you start introducing these things back into your life, do it with limitations. It defeats the purpose to just go back to your old ways immediately. Put up boundaries like: you are only allowed to go onto the internet after working hours or once you have completed everything on your to-do list. This puts limitations on when you access the internet and for how long. You can always go back and detox whenever you feel like you are being taken over by your need for the thing you are detoxing from.

Try not to go overboard with this detox. There have been some people who go as far as to remove all sources of pleasure from their lives, including talking to people and eating foods that they enjoy. This is not the right approach at all. Like I mentioned earlier, almost everything we do will release some level of dopamine, so trying to remove all sources of pleasure from your life is not going to give you the results you want. Rather, be mindful of the things that are becoming an addiction in your life and lessen your contact with that thing or remove it for a time. This is a much better way to go about dopamine detoxing.

Tricking Your Brain Into Doing Hard Things

Dopamine detoxing is meant to be done to help you do the hard things that you lack motivation to do. Many students procrastinate with their final essays because it seems like a massive task. Office employees struggle doing their year end reports because it just seems difficult and time consuming. If you do it the right way, you will see an increase in your productivity and your motivation to do these types of hard things, among others. Here are a few ways that you can use dopamine to your advantage and trick your brain into doing the hard things you often avoid.

Reward Yourself

There is nothing more motivating than a reward. It is the reason we do most things. The better the reward, the more we will want to do the task that brings us that reward. Since the things that we want the most are the things that release high amounts of dopamine, we can use those as our rewards for doing hard things. For example, if you say that you are allowed 30 minutes of internet time if you study a whole chapter of your textbook, you will be motivated to study. Not because you want to study but because you want the reward that comes after you study.

If you are going to reward yourself with highly distracting things like gaming or social media time, then you might have to structure it differently. Instead of rewarding yourself immediately, reward yourself at the end of the day. So, for every chapter you study, give yourself 30 minutes of internet time that is redeemable at the end of the day. So if you studied four chapters you have two hours that you can scroll on the internet to your heart's content. This way you are not breaking up your productive hours with distraction but you are still working towards your reward.

Listen to Music

Did you know music releases dopamine? Music can be used in conjunction with other tasks to help motivate you to do them. Tasks where you do not need complete silence to complete them can be made a lot more enjoyable by blasting some of your favorite tunes. Some people study and work better with music on but if you are not one of those people then you can stick to using music for other tasks.

Exercising, cleaning, re-organizing, and admin are all tasks that can be done with some music on. The music does not make the task more enjoyable but the music releases dopamine, which gives you the motivation you need to get the task done. This is a great hack for when you are feeling a little tired during the day as well. Music is a mood lifter so even if you only want to listen before you do the task, it can still help boost your energy levels. You can also use music as a reward as described in the above point. Just allow yourself to listen to some great music once you have completed whatever hard task you needed to get done.

Weighing up the Opportunity Cost

Opportunity cost is the value of what you have to give up in order to choose something else. There is a cost to not doing the hard things that we are supposed to, however, our brains do not register that unless we actively think about it. For instance, when we choose not to study we are choosing to not be prepared for our test and choosing to possibly fail. So, when we are supposed to study but everything in us wants us to watch another Netflix show, we are actually not choosing the most comfortable option, we are choosing to hurt ourselves in the future. When we weigh up the opportunity cost of what we are choosing to not do, we get a clear picture of what is the better choice.

When we choose the easy way out, we only think about why it is good for us now. If we were to weigh out the pros and cons of doing the hard thing vs. doing the easy thing, we would see that the easy thing is not the one that is best for us. We need to train ourselves to think like this because it is much easier to motivate yourself when you know the true value of what you are giving up. If you had a choice between watching YouTube videos or spring cleaning your house, the easiest choice is YouTube because it offers instant gratification. But if you knew that you would find $100,000 if you spring-cleaned your house, what would you choose? My guess would be that you would get right to cleaning and you would not lack the motivation to do so. This is because even though you have to do something harder, the reward is greater. If you do this when you come across a hard task, you will be able to motivate yourself to do it much easier.

Chapter 4:

Routines for Productivity

Like it or not, we are creatures of habit. Once we find something that we like, we fall into a habit and that becomes our default. If we truly want to be productive we must have the right routines in place.

You need different routines for different parts of the day because each part of the day is different and requires something different. Creating routines that make you efficient at each point will allow you to use your time efficiently. It will also let you be happier in general because you're not forcing yourself into something that is just not going to work. You will see that your day just flows better when you have the right routine in place.

When it comes to developing a routine, there's a lot of trial and error involved, so instead of giving you the exact steps I'm just going to give you an outline. It will be your job to go through and decide what is most effective for you, night and day. Every person is different so if you force someone else's routine on yourself, you might not get the results you want. If there is a specific tip that you find does not work for you, throw it out and take on something else. This is about creating YOUR most productive day.

Mornings Matter

The way we start the day sets us up for the rest of it. If you begin the day being sluggish and lazy then there is a very slim chance of us changing that in the afternoon or evening. This is the reason there has been so much emphasis on morning routines. If you get this right, the rest of the day will go much smoother.

When it comes to morning routines, there are a few things that you have to take into account. These things will help you structure your routine so that it is the most effective for you. Look at them and see if there is anything that you can improve on in your current routine.

Waking Up

Of course the most important thing about starting your morning right is actually waking up. There are many opinions floating around about what is the right time to wake up. These are all fine if they work for you, but some people don't want to wake up super early. That's okay as well. If waking up at 5am is not possible for you, then you don't have to force yourself into it. It is more important how you wake up than when you wake up in any case.

With that being said, I will say that waking up too late can be a problem. If you waste the whole morning sleeping, you will miss out on some prime productivity time. Mornings are great because the world is quieter and it gives you room to think and just be by yourself. If you live on your own then this may not be such a big problem for you. You should aim to wake up a few hours before you have to start work. If you only give yourself enough time to get ready, you will end up rushing and your day will start with you stressing and being all frazzled. Try and wake up about two hours before you have to be at work (or even earlier if you have a long commute). This will give you enough time for yourself and to do more than just get ready for work.

Once your alarm rings, get out of bed. If you can wake up without an alarm, that is even better. Our body runs on sleep cycles and when we wake up in the middle of one of these cycles, we wake up groggy, even if we got a full night of sleep. There are plenty of apps out there that help track your sleep cycles so that you wake up at the best time for you. If you wake up at the same time every day then your body will pick up on this and eventually, you won't need an alarm clock. This is the most ideal way to wake up. This does mean that you will have to wake up the same time every day, including the weekends. Don't break the routine, your body will thank you for it.

Eliminate Decision Making

We all have a limited amount of decision-making power each day. Using it up too early in the morning is a really bad idea, since the big decisions will probably only come later in the day. In the morning our decisions are what to wear, what to have for breakfast, or what to pack for lunch. In the grand scheme of things, these are really inconsequential decisions. Instead of wasting your decision-making ability on those things, save it for more important things.

Inevitably, you will have to be making these trivial morning decisions at some point. The trick is to do it at night before bed. You can make easy decisions at night and this will form part of an effective night-time routine. We will speak more about this later on in the chapter.

Move a Little

Nobody is saying that you have to do a full-on hour workout first thing in the morning, but it definitely does help if you do some kind of physical activity. It will wake up your body and get your blood flowing. You will find that you are more alert and awake afterwards.

Along with the movement, remember to hydrate. You haven't had anything to drink the whole night and you are probably dehydrated. This is the reason many people feel tired in the morning. Boost your metabolism and give yourself an energy boost with a glass of cold water in the mornings before you get to exercising. Remember to choose an exercise that you enjoy doing!

Get Your Mind in the Zone

If you are able to get your mind focused from the beginning of the day, you won't struggle with this as the day progresses. The basic structure of getting your mind in the zone should be to do something you enjoy, gratitude, plan for the day, and learn something. These four things form a foundation for a successful day. They each help refocus your mind on what is important and it will carry you through the rest of the day.

These four things might seem like a lot, but they don't actually take that much time at all. Doing something you enjoy could be going for a walk, cuddling your dog, reading a bit of your favorite book or blog, or anything else that makes you happy. Depending on the time you have available this can be 5 to 20 minutes in the morning. From here, you can move straight into gratitude. Many people use this as a time to meditate. The goal is to think about all the things you do have, because it is difficult to be in a bad mood when you are so thankful for all that you have. The next thing is to plan for your day. Think about what you will need to get done today. What are your top goals for the day? Writing them down will solidify them and motivate you to get them done. This will possibly only take a few minutes.

Last thing on the list is to learn something. The morning is probably the best time to take in new information. Our minds are clear and awake so new information just seeps in. Taking 10 to 20 minutes to read a book or listen to a podcast is a great way to expand your knowledge. You can even do this during the commute to work. Switch on a podcast and just see what you can learn. You never know what new perspectives you could gain from just giving a few minutes a day to learning something new.

You don't have to do these things in order, do whatever works for you. Some of these things can be combined if you are tight on time. The thing you enjoy and your learning thing could be reading something new. Mold it to your lifestyle

Do the Hard Thing

This step is not actually part of your morning routine but it should be the first thing you do in a work context. Technically, it will still be in the morning so that is why it is included. If you have a difficult task for the day, do it first. This is the time where your willpower is highest and you are able to give your tasks the most attention. We all know that when the day wears on, things get a little crazy and there are interruptions coming from every side. If you have already done the hardest thing of the day, you know that you have accomplished something big. This feeling will motivate you for the rest of the work day.

The thing with the big important tasks is that we don't want to do them. Those are the things we procrastinate on. Those tasks are also the reason we feel so unproductive when the day is done. Even if it is the absolute worst thing in the world, at least you know that it is behind you and there is nothing else that could possibly be worse. Your day will just improve from there. It also won't be the end of the world if the day takes an unexpected turn and you end up having to throw out the daily plan.

The Afternoon Slump

This is the worst time of the day for productivity. It is usually around 1pm to 3pm, after lunch. Your willpower is at an all-time low and you don't want to do anything. At this point, most employees are just counting down the hours until they can pack up and leave.

The reason for the afternoon slump is that our bodies naturally have a strong urge to sleep between the hours of 1pm and 3pm. This is a natural process and the reason many countries enjoy siestas (napping during the afternoon). This tired feeling is worsened by stress, dehydration, and just being drained from the work day. So if you feel like it is just you, everyone feels a little sluggish during the afternoon. The good news is that there are actions you can do to make your afternoons productive.

Having a set-in-stone routine for the afternoon can be a bit difficult since every day can bring something new. The middle of the workday is often the most unpredictable or the least consistent. The best you can do is have a system to organize your tasks and fit them in the best places during the day. The goal is to create a sort of structure that you can follow during the afternoons that will allow you to be as productive as you were in the morning.

Eat the Right Lunch

If you want to have energy throughout the afternoon, you are going to have to eat a nutritious lunch that will fuel you. If you eat a large meal that is high in fat and sugars, you will feel lethargic and your slump will be worsened. Lunch is often people's most unhealthiest meal because they are so hungry that they start craving the unhealthy foods that are quickly available. If you are going to eat a pizza washed down with some soda, you will definitely suffer from an afternoon crash.

Make sure that you prepare a healthy, filling meal in advance. You also need to watch the portion size. Too much food (even if it's healthy) can make you feel lethargic. Pack a healthy lunch as well as some energy boosting snacks to munch on throughout the day so when lunchtime rolls around you are not starving. Also make sure that you are drinking enough water throughout the day. Lunchtime is the perfect opportunity to catch up on your water intake if you have been lacking.

Actually Take Your Break

There is a very bad habit that is going around the corporate world where people just don't take their lunch breaks. It may sound noble or you may seem like a hard worker when you do this but the truth is that it is actually doing more harm than good. People are not robots and working eight to nine hours flat is not good for us. The break is there for a reason.

The best thing you can do in your break is to get a change of scenery. Go outside and get some fresh air while you enjoy your lunch. Take this time to clear your mind. You can do something you enjoy like read or listen to music. That sort of thing replenishes you and gives your mind a chance to renew itself. Try to disconnect as much as you can from work while you are on the break.

Do the Easier Tasks

If you followed the productive morning routine suggestion then the hardest part of your work should be done. What is left is the easier, more mundane things. Unfortunately, no matter how much we try, we will be more worn down in the afternoon. It is just something that happens so instead of forcing ourselves to do things that are energy intensive, plan the day so that the things that use less brain power are left for the afternoons.

If you plan your days effectively then you will be able to get the most amount of work done. Try getting to emails and scheduling meetings in the afternoons. These tasks don't use a lot of energy so you don't have to be on the top of your game to do them. Planning for the next day and tying up loose ends can also be done towards the end of the day. This will help you have everything ready for the next day and it will feel like you accomplished what you set out to do for the day.

Productive Evenings

A productive day actually starts the night before. Evening routines are just as important as morning routines, even though they don't get as much attention. The things you do in the evening can actually determine whether the next day is as productive as you would like it to be. The problem is that as soon as people get home, they just want to unwind so they eat dinner and waste the rest of the evening watching Netflix. While there is nothing wrong with unwinding and watching your favorite shows, sometimes we overdo it. We could be using the time to actually set ourselves up well for the next day and if we are smart about it, we can get the rest we need.

The following are just elements of an effective night-time routine. If you can implement them daily, you will see a difference in how you feel in the morning and how you sleep at night. The goal of evening routines are to relax, unplug, prepare for the next day, and get a good night's sleep. Your evening routine will only take place after you have eaten, taken care of the kids, and completed any evening chores. Once all that is done, it is time to focus on yourself. If you have a spouse, remember to make time for them as well.

Do Something You Enjoy

Throughout the day you were probably not focused on yourself. You were attending to your boss, your clients, and your employees. The evening is the time where you get to do something for you. If you have a hobby this is the perfect time to do it. You need some time for yourself, where you can just switch off. Preferably this does not include binging on your favorite shows.

If you don't have a hobby then you should find one. You can be productive in areas apart from work. Hobbies and clubs allow you to explore your other interests and help you to grow in other areas. Essentially, you are becoming a more well-rounded person when your life consists of more than just work and home responsibilities.

Evenings are also a great time to exercise if you didn't get a chance to do it during the day. Many people go to the gym, play a sport, or simply go for a run. It is a great way to let off steam and put your energy into something else. You will also feel better after getting your body moving.

Plan for Tomorrow

After all your responsibilities have been taken care of, it is time to plan for the next day. This planning includes meal prepping and setting out your clothes for tomorrow. Remember in the morning routine section we spoke about not making too many decisions in the morning? Well, making those decisions the night before is the way you do that.

Remember to make healthy meal choices. You can prepare breakfast and lunch to give yourself more time in the mornings. Taking out your clothes will allow you to make a smooth transition from the bed to getting ready without having to stop and decide what to wear.

This time is also great to sit down and plan out the activities you want to get done for the next day. Some people prefer to do this in the morning, but the evening works just as well. You can also spend some time reflecting on how the day went. Think about what went well and what can be improved upon. This is an active way for you to keep improving every day. Journaling is a great tool for this. It will also help you get out any thoughts and put it on paper. You will see how much less you think or worry about things once they are out of your head and onto the paper. This will help with the winding down process.

Get Ready for Bed

Getting a good night's sleep is highly dependent on the actions you take before you actually fall asleep. Oftentimes we get into bed and try and fall asleep but our thoughts are racing so we find it difficult to doze off. Even worse is we get into bed and watch YouTube videos or scroll through social media for so long that we don't even feel tired anymore. We can end up staying up way later than we intend to.

If we don't have a good, restful night's sleep we will not be able to function at our best in the morning. Sleep should be a priority for all of us and it doesn't have to be a struggle every night. Creating a good routine is the first step and sticking to it is the second. Once you have completed everything you wanted to for the evening, start a bedtime routine. This will be the exact same every night so that your body knows it's time to wind down. Find something that works for you. For example, your routine could look something like: drink a cup of tea, brush teeth, read for 20 minutes, go to sleep. If you consistently do these things every time you are getting ready for bed, your body will take that as a bedtime cue. It will be far easier to fall asleep if your body recognizes this.

Another big thing that you must do if you really want a good night's sleep is to put away all technology 30 minutes to an hour before going to bed. That is phones, laptops, tablets, TVs, and anything else that has a light-up screen. The light emitted from these devices tricks the body into believing it is still daytime, which is why so many people struggle to fall asleep when they're on their phones. Our bodies are designed to sleep when it gets dark so if that never happens it can be a challenge to fall asleep quickly. It should definitely not take you hours of lying in bed before you fall asleep.

Reading is a far better thing to do before bed. You could read a physical b0ok or on an e-reader. I would not suggest reading on your phone, even if you do put it on night mode, you can still easily get distracted by messages and notifications. It really doesn't matter what you read, fiction or nonfiction, pick something you enjoy. You will find your eyes starting to get heavy and you will be able to fall asleep a few moments after you put the book down and set your head on the pillow. Your sleep quality will improve, which will improve how you feel the next day.

Chapter 5:

Managing Your Energy and Attention

There are lots of books and articles out there about managing time but not many about managing your attention and energy. I would argue that these two aspects are even more important than managing your time. No matter how much time you have, you will never be able to do anything if your energy is low or if you are not able to give attention to the task at hand. This is why so many people struggle with time management.

We all have the same number of hours in the day. No matter what we do, we can never get more than that, yet there are some people who seem to get so much more done in that time than others. They are not special, nor have some secret time-managing formula. These people are the ones who know how to manage their energy and attention. So, let's learn how to become one of those people.

Managing Your Energy

Let's first touch on managing energy. Unfortunately, this is one resource that is constantly depleted. People think that they can run for a long period of time on low energy levels but eventually they burn out. The long and the short of it is that we need energy in order for us to do things. Trying to beat this system only hurts ourselves and our productivity in the long term.

The most productive people are those that are able to get the most of whatever time they have. Time is not the limiting factor. Once you realize this you will be able to shift your mind onto managing your energy instead. Our full potential relies on the energy required to get there.

The Four Kinds of Energy

Energy can be found in four different areas of our lives. We should be mindful of all four of these areas. If we know which of these areas are lacking, we can focus on bringing that level up. These four areas are physical, emotional, spiritual, and mental energy. Let's dive into them a little bit more:

Physical Energy

This is listed first because it is the basis of all the other types of energy. Naturally, if we do not have the physical energy to do something, the other energy types won't really matter that much. Physical energy has to do with your body and how healthy it is. Even though it is important to us, it is the one type that is neglected the most. People tend to push themselves over their physical limits and then end up so fatigued that they are unhappy, depressed, and start suffering from a whole host of health issues.

The three things that affect our physical energy the most are nutrition, fitness, and sleep. I'm sure you can pick out at least one of these things that you have been neglecting. Even though they are so important to our well-being these three areas of our lives are the first we let go off when life gets a bit stressful. We start binge eating, skipping the gym, and start staying awake longer to finish whatever task we need to get done.

Emotional Energy

Emotional energy is defined by how well we handle our emotions. If we are a positive person who looks on the bright side, then our emotional energy is high. On the flip side, if we are constantly agitated, angry, frustrated, or overwhelmed then there is a good chance that our emotional energy is off balance.

When our emotional energy is low, we tend to react to things in a bad way. We have a low tolerance for inconveniences and things that cause stress. There will definitely be times when your emotional energy runs low, like big projects, exams, and many situations where people are counting on you, but you should not always be running on empty. Usually, the people around you will be able to tell if you are emotionally drained before you notice it. Emotional energy is not something we often keep tabs on because we don't link emotions to feelings of fatigue. If you find yourself acting out of character or being short with people, it might be time to self-reflect and check on your emotional energy.

Spiritual Energy

This type of energy is tied to the feeling of purpose we get when we do something. Each one of us wants to do something or be part of something that gives us purpose. We want to be fulfilled by the things we spend our time on. If our work is not fulfilling us we can struggle to get this form of energy filled up. This is especially so if we are doing something that goes against our values and beliefs.

If you are a religious person then your religion would also play a big part here. You would have a certain belief structure and anything that compromises that puts you in a tough spot. This is very conflicting and can cause some internal struggles. If you are not living according to your values and beliefs, your spiritual energy can go way down and could manifest itself as you being drained and unmotivated.

Mental Energy

Mental energy is focused on what is going on inside your mind. So many people suffer from mental fog. If you cannot think clearly then there is no way that you will be productive. Your mind has to be sharp in order for you to plan, prepare, and complete the tasks you need to. If you find yourself constantly drifting off or not being able to concentrate on one thing for a good amount of time, then your mental energy could be depleted.

Our mentality doesn't just affect our mind, eventually it starts to creep into our relationships, work ethics, and physical health. There has been a rise in awareness of the importance of mental health. This is because we can see the effects of depression and anxiety. It seems like this is increasing at a rapid pace. It is not good for us to be in a negative mental space. A healthy mindset is one that is positive and that looks for solutions to problems instead of being crippled by them.

Increasing Your Energy Levels

There are things you can do to get more energy in the short-term, caffeine is one of them. However, whatever quick fixes you try will not get to the root of the problem and will probably do more bad than good in the long-term.

Physical Energy

We have already spoken about the three main areas of physical energy being nutrition, fitness, and sleep. Now we need to see how we can increase overall physical energy by improving each of these areas. Of course, all of these areas are important to your physical energy but they need different things from you to help find balance. So, we will be focusing on each one. Make sure that you don't neglect one because they all affect each other in some way. The only way to have optimum physical energy is to have all of these areas in top condition.

Let's talk about nutrition first. The food we eat fuels our bodies, it is the most basic form of energy. We need good fuel to sustain us for long periods of time and prevent us from crashing early on in the day. The goal of having the right nutrition is to stabilize our blood sugar levels. When we eat something that is not healthy, heavily processed, or high in sugar, it spikes our blood sugar and then it drops again very quickly. This is what gives us those energy spikes and crashes. We should aim to eat foods that will release energy slowly and sustainably. This is how we fuel our bodies for the whole day.

In order for you to eat these healthy foods you have to have them available. So, it's time to take a look in your grocery cupboard and do a thorough clean out of everything that is not good for you. Moving towards whole foods or ones that are minimally processed are the best options. Foods high in protein and healthy carbs burn slower and keep you fuller for longer. Also remember to get a good amount of fresh fruit and veggies in your diet. Your body needs a balanced diet to function properly.

The next thing we should focus on is fitness. Our level of fitness determines how well we transport oxygen throughout our bodies. As you know, oxygen is extremely important for us to live. Increased oxygen transport means more energy and we are able to sustain ourselves for much longer. People who don't exercise regularly are more at risk of feeling sluggish and lethargic throughout the day. This hurts our productivity. Why do you think most of the productivity gurus are in such good shape? This definitely does not mean that you have to be ripped to be productive but you do have to have a decent fitness level. So, if you get winded playing with children or taking a brisk walk then it is time to up your fitness level.

Unfortunately, the only way to do this is to exercise. Exercising is one of the most hated and avoided actions in our society today. People are always too quick to come up with excuses as to why they can't commit to it. The most common excuse being not having enough time. Look, you really don't have to exercise for two hours every day to be healthy. Just 30 minutes three times a week. If you were really honest with yourself you would be able to fit this in somewhere. Maybe don't watch that rerun of Friends for the 15th time? Start small and then build yourself up, even 5 minutes of exercise is better than nothing. Find something you enjoy doing and stick to it.

The last thing that helps increase physical energy is sleep. Sleep is literally resting and recharging your body. There is no way that you would be able to be effective if you don't sleep enough. Also, catching up sleep on the weekends is not a real thing. Sleep doesn't work on an average per week because you can't carry it over to the next day. You have to be getting a good amount of sleep every single day. Get your seven to eight hours of good quality sleep at night and you will almost immediately notice an increase in your energy levels and alertness.

Emotional Energy

Emotional energy can be a tough one to gain back quickly. If you are feeling emotionally drained, it helps to figure out what the cause is and counteract that. Remember that emotions carry over into all areas of your life, so if you are upset about something that happened at home, you will still feel those emotions when you get to work. There will always be things that play on your emotions but a true mark of emotional stability is if those things don't cripple you. You should still be able to continue with your daily tasks and look for the bright side of the situation.

People also play a big part in our emotional energy. Some people drain us and others lift our spirits and give us energy. This is why it is important to have the right people around you. If you notice that someone is a constant downer or their presence drains you, then try and not be in their presence often. Pick friends who lift you up and who you enjoy being around. You are under no obligation to be in the company of people who bring you down. We often take on the energy of the people we are around. So even if you are a person who has a negative outlook on things it will do you some good to keep the company of positive people.

When it comes to emotional energy it could also help to understand whether you are an introvert or extrovert. This has nothing to do with if you like people or not. It also has nothing to do with if you are shy or not.

Extroverts get their energy from being around people, while introverts get their energy from being on their own. Both groups need people but in different quantities. If an extrovert is feeling down they will seek out people. If an introvert is feeling down they would rather be by themselves, but once their energy is up they do enjoy the company of others. Knowing which category you fall into can help you decide what you need to do when you are feeling a bit drained. Whether you are an introvert or an extrovert, you will need the right people around you. Both need positive friends and family that they enjoy being around.

Spiritual Energy

If you are passionate about what you do and you find purpose in it you will have energy for it. Sometimes our jobs just don't fulfill us in that way. If you can find a job that truly fulfills you and aligns with your core values then you should definitely stick with it. If you do not have one of these kinds of jobs you will have to try and fulfill yourself in other areas. This can be a tough one since your work is where you will be spending a majority of your time. With that being said, it does not necessarily have to be a place where you draw your purpose from.

The first thing you have to do is figure out what you are passionate about. I know this can be a tough question to answer for some but it is definitely worth doing some introspection to find out. There are things that you really enjoy and if you haven't found those as of yet it can be really fun and fulfilling to try different things until you get to the thing that you truly love doing. Start by volunteering and doing things for other people. When we do things for others it fulfills us. We can so often get caught up in our own lives that we forget that there are problems in the world that we have the resources to change.

If you are a religious person, get connected to your religion. Life sometimes gets busy and we can forget to connect back to what we truly believe. Go back to the start and surround yourself with like-minded people who share your same core values. This will help guide you and keep you on the path you need to be on. Religion and faith are a big part of many people's lives and it can drain you if you are not as connected as you used to be.

Mental Energy

You will know that your mental energy is high when you have a clear mind, are able to concentrate on the tasks in front of you, and have the habit of positive thinking. If you are constantly down, suffer from a mental fog, or just feel flustered all the time then it is very possible that your mental energy is depleted. You would feel as though you don't have space in your mind for more information and you aren't able to sort through everything effectively. This sort of thing happens to most people at least a few times, so you are not alone.

If you want to increase your mental energy you have to learn to clear your mind. This can be difficult in this digital age. Information is being thrown at us at such a speed that we hardly have time to sort through it. Practicing mindfulness is a great way for us to disconnect and refresh our minds. Mindfulness is just taking some time to pause and just slow down your mind. It gives you time to sort through thoughts, feelings, and experiences. You get to ask yourself why you are feeling a certain way or introspect to why you reacted to a situation in a specific way. This kind of slowing down is exactly what our minds need. Even if you don't necessarily think of anything during this time, that's perfectly fine. Our minds need a break too.

People have found great success in doing deep breathing exercises to clear their minds. Another thing that works is to remove yourself from the situation that is stressing you out or making you feel overwhelmed. This is not about running away from your problems but rather about taking a step back to refresh your perspective. Once you take that step back, you will be able to look at the situation in a different light. Taking a walk and getting some fresh air is sometimes all you need. Again, I will reiterate how important it is to have the right people around you. Make sure the people you surround yourself with are uplifting and can help you out of mental blocks rather than people who bring you down and only look at the negatives. It is so important to protect your mental health, don't let other people be the reason you are losing mental energy.

Renewing Your Energy Throughout the Day

As the day wears on, we can hit slumps in our energy. These slumps are sometimes not caused by a major lack in one of the areas mentioned above, instead it is just a case of needing a boost or renewal of energy. When we are doing monotonous or stressful tasks, it can sap our energy. Hopefully, you aren't doing these types of tasks all the time but they can't be completely avoided. If you find yourself feeling a bit drained and your energy has been depleted, you need to have a plan on how to give yourself a little increase in energy. Thankfully, it doesn't have to take much.

Take a Nap

There have been many studies that show mid-day naps boost moods and productivity. It is a time to really switch off and rest before moving on with the rest of the day. This can be difficult in an office environment, but if you are able to get a quick 20-minute nap in, then you should. Close the door to your office or go to your car and get some shut eye. If you work for yourself or work from home this will be easier for you, so take a break and lay down for a short while. Once you wake up, drink some water to refresh yourself and you should be good to go for the next few hours.

Get Some Fresh Air

Sometimes all we need is a change in scenery and to get away. Getting some fresh air and some sun might be just what you need. You would be amazed at how refreshed you feel after you have taken some time to walk outside. It is even better if you take your lunch break outside. Let your mind wander and don't think about work during this time, enjoy it.

Meditate

There are many people who are skeptical about meditation. This is probably because it has some sort of spiritual stigma. It does not have to mean saying a specific mantra or anything like that. In fact, meditation can look different for everyone. You can listen to a guided meditation (there are plenty of apps, podcasts, and Youtube videos that do these) or you could simply just sit still and listen to yourself breathing. The point is to slow down your mind and give it a break from everything it was thinking about throughout the day.

Read or Listen to Something Inspiring

Sometimes all we need is a new perspective and an inspiring book or podcast can help with that. It also helps to take your mind off the work you are currently doing and focus on something else completely. You could read or listen to something funny or just interesting as well. Try to keep away from social media and the internet in general. Books and podcasts are your best bet since there is less of a chance for you to be distracted and landing up in some internet rabbit hole.

Choose what you will read or listen to beforehand. This will eliminate you having to scroll through and find something worthwhile. You can do this on your lunch break. Reading or listening to an audiobook will give your mind a break from your work. You also never know what you will learn that you could implement at some point in the future. This is just a good habit to implement into your daily life.

Do Something Fun

We are often drained because we are doing work that is hard and sometimes we just don't enjoy the tasks that we have to do. To break this up, choose to use your break to do something you enjoy. Nobody said you can't have a little fun during the work day. Take a walk. Eat at your favorite restaurant. Work on a hobby. Find a way to bring something you enjoy to your working environment and pull it out when you feel a bit drained.

Doing something fun is a great way to take a break. Too often we take breaks to just eat and we don't enjoy the time. This is an inefficient way to take a break. It is called a break for a reason; you should be able to completely break away from your work for a little while. You will find that you are refreshed and have much more energy to tackle the rest of the day once you do this.

Call a Friend

Sometimes all we need is a friendly voice or someone to talk to. Take a break to chat to a friend and catch up with them. We already know that relationships are important and this is a great way to cultivate your relationships and get your energy levels up. Remember to call someone who is positive and who will lift your mood. Don't call someone who will want something from you or will end up bringing you down. The goal is to have a fun, lighthearted conversation or to vent if you need to. There is a time and a place to talk about personal problems or ask for favors and this is not it.

It is a good idea to let your friends know that you might be calling them when you just want to chat and have a break from work. Make sure that they know that they can do the same to you. This also sets up the expectation for the phone call. Both parties will know what to expect from the call and hopefully both will leave feeling better.

Managing Your Attention

Just like time, our attention is a limited resource. We can't make more of it so when it is done, it is done. This means that we need to know where to spend our attention so that we can be the most productive. Attention is a powerful tool that can help us get further in our lives, but, if used on the wrong things, can have the opposite effect. At the end of the day, what we pay attention to is what will manifest itself in our lives.

If we pay attention to the work we are doing, it will get done. If we pay attention to things that are not important, we will live in a state of constant distraction and never do anything productive with ourselves. This is why where you focus your attention is far more important than how much time you have. A focused mind can get things done in half the time of that of a distracted mind.

Attention is the ability to focus on one thing while ignoring all other stimuli. It can actually shape how we see things around us and how we experience the world. We decide what we give our attention to, whether that is consciously or subconsciously. This is also the reason three people can be in the same room, witness the same situation but all give different renditions of what happened. It all comes down to where their attention lies.

As much as we would like to think that we can concentrate on many things at once, we just simply cannot. If we do try to focus on too much, we never truly focus on anything and our brain is split in too many directions. Like I mentioned earlier, attention is a finite resource. So you have the choice to focus on one thing and get it done as quickly and efficiently as possible, or you can try and focus on many things by giving small pieces of your attention to each. Essentially, it will take you longer to complete those tasks and you can easily get confused and overwhelmed.

The Two Types of Attention

There are two types of attention out there. The first is voluntary attention and the second is involuntary attention. Knowing the difference between the two will help manage your attention better.

Voluntary Attention

When we think about giving our attention to something, this is the type of attention we are thinking about. We have conscious control over this type of attention and therefore choose where we put that attention. We use our will power to place our attention on something that we want to concentrate on. We need this kind of attention to block out all other stimuli and focus on what we need to get done. What we spend our voluntary attention on is usually what we will be productive in.

It can be difficult to call upon this type of attention when there are lots of things around us that are distracting. As much as paying attention to something is an act of will power, there is only so much will power we have. As soon as we add a distraction to the mix we make it harder for us to give our attention to the things we need to. This is why we prefer to work and study in quiet areas or put our phones on silent when we are busy with something important.

Everything amazing around us was built using voluntary attention. Beautiful pieces of art that took years to complete, the inspiring and entertaining stories we read, the masterpieces of architecture all over our cities, the TV shows we watch, and the technology we enjoy were all birthed out of someone's voluntary attention. Unfortunately, the world we live in today makes it harder for us to tap into our voluntary attention. It takes a lot more conscious effort from us to really get into a state where we can give our full attention to something.

Involuntary Attention

Involuntary attention is the type of attention that we don't consciously control. It is controlled by the things going on around us. Think about when you hear a loud noise, someone calls your name, or when you just notice something out of the ordinary. You don't continuously say "I am going to concentrate on that thing," but your mind is already there. This type of attention is what usually distracts us from giving our voluntary attention to things that are important.

Involuntary attention is not all bad. In fact, it does perform an important function in our lives. We need it when we are in danger or need to quickly bring our attention to something. If we did not have involuntary attention, we would be so focused on the tasks in front of us that we wouldn't flinch if, say, the fire alarm went off. Sometimes we do need our attention to be taken away from the things we are focusing on. The problem is that there is too much external stimulation. Our minds are always in the involuntary attention stage. This is really bad for our productivity.

With all that being said, if we use involuntary stimulation in the right way it can give our minds the break it needs. We can quiet the mind and let it focus on what it wants to focus on. Think about when you are out for a walk in nature, you are not consciously focusing on anything. Instead, you are just letting your attention be pulled in whatever direction it wants to be. When used in this way involuntary attention can relieve stress and rejuvenate the mind.

Focused Attention

Under the umbrella of voluntary attention is focused attention. This dictates how you use your voluntary attention to focus on a certain thing. The two types are narrow-focused and broad-focused attention. They are used in different situations. It is not too important to go in-depth into this subject but you should have a basic understanding of it. This way, you will be able to know which type you will need to use to be effective in certain situations.

Narrow focus is when you are concentrating on one specific task. It allows you to pour all your attention into this one thing. You don't really have to consider other aspects around you. It helps when you have a difficult or meticulous task to get done. It is not good to be narrow-focused when you are dealing with other people or have larger tasks to do and plan for. Narrow focus can create a tunnel vision and make it difficult to take in other areas for consideration.

Broad focus gives you a wider perspective. You focus more on the bigger picture and can deal with complex issues. Bigger projects do need you to use broad focus, especially in the planning stages. On the other hand, having a broad focus can be a bad thing when you have to get down into the details of things. If you are working with budgets, accounting, and intricate tasks, then having a broad focus could be a hindrance.

Broad and narrow focus can be explained a bit better using an example. Think of a game of baseball. When the fielder gets into position and begins the game, he has to have a broad focus. He takes in everything that is happening so that he is aware of the entire game. He makes sure he knows where the other players are situated so that if he has to catch the ball he knows exactly what to do with it. As soon as the batter hits the ball, his focus shifts into narrow focus. The fielder must keep his attention on the ball so that he can catch it. Once it is in his hands, he shifts again to broad focus to see where he needs to throw the ball before shifting again to narrow focus to calculate the best way to throw the ball to get it into the baseman's hands.

When it comes to baseball, this shifting needs to happen in a matter of seconds. Hopefully, this example has shown you how each of these types of focuses help productivity in different situations. In everyday life, we do not have to switch between the two so quickly. We just have to understand which tasks fit into which category so we can plan for it. In general, tasks that require narrow focus need a lot more attention, as they drain a person much quicker. The best time to do these tasks is when you have the most energy and your attention is at its peak. Broader-focused tasks can be left until later because they do not require as much intense attention.

How to Manage Attention Effectively

Now that we know a bit more about attention and why it is important, the next thing we need to understand is how to manage this attention properly. When we break our focus, it takes time to get back in the zone. This is a whole bunch of wasted time. Some studies have shown that it takes about 30 minutes for you to gain back your focus after you have gotten distracted. That is 30 minutes of not really doing anything because you are trying to guide your mind back to what it is supposed to be doing.

The first thing you should do is make sure that you limit the amount of distractions around you. Distractions are the thief of attention. You don't want to shift from voluntary attention to involuntary attention multiple times while you are performing an important task. Understand what distracts you and then remove it. If it is other people that keep interrupting you, make a sign and put it on your desk so that people know not to disturb you during this time. You could also listen to some white noise to drown out all other sounds. There are a plethora of things you can do to eliminate distractions once you know what those distractions are.

You should also take some time to find out when your attention is at its highest. Some people find they focus better in the mornings, while others prefer the evenings. If you are not sure which you are, take a few days to track yourself. Write down when you were most productive and when you started feeling a bit sluggish and found it hard to concentrate. Track your distractions, what distracted you, and at which times these distractions were at their worst. Once you have this information, you can decide when is the best time to do each task. If you are most attentive in the morning then use this time to focus on tasks that require a lot more meticulous attention. These would be your narrow focus tasks. As the day goes on and your attention starts wavering, you can move over to the broad-focused tasks that don't need as much attention. This way, you will be able to structure your day in a way that is the most effective for you.

The key to managing your attention is making sure you prioritize the right tasks at the right time. Like I said earlier, attention is finite and you can't make more of it. This is why spending that attention on the things that are most in need of it is crucial. Don't waste your focus on easy tasks, rather, do the most difficult ones when your attention is at its maximum level.

Chapter 6:

Hack Your Productivity

Sometimes all we need is a simple hack to get us out of a slump or improve our productivity just that extra bit. Not all of these will work for everyone but there are definitely some good tips in this chapter. Go through it and find the ones that will work best for you. Perhaps you can try a few every week until you find the perfect ones for your lifestyle.

Don't feel discouraged if one of them does not work out for you. Remember what we spoke about in Chapter 2? Everyone is different and that means that it's okay for different things to work for different people. Try some of these out and I'm sure you will find the perfect hacks for you.

Set One Goal for the Day

This hack is about breaking the habit of multitasking. We have already touched on why multitasking is bad. The simple fact is that humans were not built for multitasking. Instead, if we focus on one task at a time, we are able to do it well and finish it in a good amount of time.

All you have to do is pick one thing that you would like to get done that day. You can then break it up into smaller tasks. If you are only focused on one thing your full attention is given to it. Even if there are smaller tasks involved in the completion of the overall goal, your attention is still never divided between multiple things. Everything is interconnected and you can see how the smaller tasks help complete the bigger one.

The Pomodoro Technique

The Pomodoro Technique is basically working in short bursts and then taking short breaks before getting back into work. You work for 25 minutes and then take a 5-minute break. You repeat this process a few times before you need to take your regular longer break.

There are many studies out there that state that people can't concentrate for long periods of time. In fact, this time is getting shorter and shorter now that we are living in the fast moving digital age. There has not been any conclusive number as to how long humans can concentrate for. Some studies suggest only 10 to 15 minutes, while others near the 30-minute mark. However, what we do know is that trying to concentrate on one thing for hours does not work.

You may have to experiment with the times and see what kind of intervals work for you. The breaks shouldn't be too long, just a short break to focus on something else and give your mind some down time. Try using this time to get away from your work completely. Taking a 5-minute walk is a great way to use your break time. You could also use this time to reward yourself for the work you have done. Play your favorite game, get a snack, scroll social media, or just go out and get some fresh air. Whatever you choose to do in your break make sure that you only do it for the allocated break time. If you know you will get caught up on social media for more than the time you set out then that should not be part of your break.

Regular Breaks

This basically rides off the previous point. You have to be taking frequent breaks. Don't push yourself to concentrate for so long that you absolutely can't anymore. If you do that, you risk not being able to focus on your work for the rest of the day. If you feel your mind drifting off then this is a sign that you need to take a break. Remove yourself from the situation and clear your mind. After a few minutes, you will be ready to take on the task with a refreshed mind. This is far more effective than trying to push through a mental block or forcing yourself to work until you can't anymore.

Create a Workspace

This is especially important if you work from home. Having a dedicated workspace allows you to have somewhere to work and have somewhere to leave once you are done working. It almost causes your brain to switch from work mode to rest mode and vice versa.

Many people work on their beds when they work from home but this is one of the worst things you can do. When you do this your brain does not see the bedroom as a place of rest so you might find that you struggle to fall asleep or to leave your work when the work day is over. This lack of boundaries can lead to fatigue and burnout.

If you are a freelancer or just generally work outside of an office environment, then having a dedicated workspace outside from your recreational and resting places is crucial. You can create a little home office, go to a coffee shop, or utilize a co-working space. Doing this will allow you to get focused when you need to be focused and leave work when you need to.

Task Management Tools

I know I have said a lot about the downside to technology in terms of productivity, but there are plenty of apps and tools that are very useful. If you use the right task management tool, your productivity could really improve. There are different types so there is sure to be one that fits your needs.

Some of them are pretty simple. You can just create to-do lists and just make general breakdowns of your tasks. Others offer more, like trackers and the ability to link with other members of your team. A few suggestions of these kinds of tools are Monday and Trello.

Share Your Goals and Work as a Team

If you have a specific goal in mind then share it with someone. Let them keep you accountable and maybe even help you with it. A study in 2014 stated that sharing your goals and working with a team increased productivity (Brooks, 2020). We are social beings and there is just something about working with people that helps us be more efficient.

Even if you are not all working on the same thing, having someone there with you will keep you motivated. If you see other people working hard you will want to as well. This is why study groups are so helpful. Most of the time you are not talking to the people you are studying with but their presence helps you stay focused. This can be the same for work situations. Find a team that will keep you accountable and motivated.

Schedule Your Meetings Effectively

In most jobs, clubs, and basically anything that involves a group of people, meetings are standard. There is no getting away from it but you need to make sure you are scheduling your meetings effectively throughout the day. Having your meetings all over the place will mean that you are constantly being interrupted. Anything that you try and get done during the day will have to be split up into small work sections and that is not always effective. And if we are being honest, no one actually feels super motivated or productive after sitting through a long meeting.

The best thing you can do is to schedule your meeting into one block of time. if you have two or three meetings in the day, try to schedule them around the same time so that you can be in and out of meetings for a specific time. The rest of the day can be focused on doing the rest of your work. You can decide when this is more effective for you. You could schedule your meeting first thing in the morning or later on in the day when you have gotten the bulk of your work done. Decide how you want to do it and let the rest of your staff, customers, or co-workers know the plan going forward.

Of course, there are sometimes last-minute meetings that have to be attended to. Sometimes, these cannot be avoided but this is not the norm. As long as you are able to stick to this type of scheduling, for the most part you will still reap the benefits. If it is possible to have days where there are no meetings at all, that would be ideal. Some companies have set up things like "No Meeting Wednesdays" to boost productivity and to allow staff to have ample time to finish their work. Adopting something similar in your own life could also be very beneficial.

Don't Have Meetings for the Sake of It

Have you ever attended a meeting and left thinking, "that could have been an email"? I think most of us have attended our fair share of unnecessary meetings. It can be really draining and time consuming to be in a meeting that has no benefit to you. I'm not sure why people think it necessary to have meetings every day but it is the current work culture and it is not effective.

Meetings definitely help to get people on the same page, flesh out ideas, or try and develop new solutions. The first problem is that there are often people in meetings that don't need to be there. The second is that there are just too many unnecessary meetings being held. You really don't need daily check-up meetings where people go on about what they are going to be busy with during the day. Think about it. Say you have six people in the meeting sharing for five minutes each about what they will be doing during the day. You have wasted 25 minutes of each person's time because they have to sit and listen to their colleagues go on about things that are of no consequence to them.

There are easier and more efficient ways to get information from people. If you are a team manager, consider asking your team to send an email with their plan for the day before they get to work. Also, make sure that when you do have a meeting that you have something important to say. If used correctly, meetings can be a powerful tool to inspire people, create solutions, and birth new ideas.

When You Are Done, Switch Off

In 2020 we have seen many people working from home and many people feeling overworked and fatigued. Many would have assumed that working from home was less stressful and you could possibly work less than you did in the office. What happened was the complete opposite. People did not know when to switch off. Instead of working their regular eight hours, employees were clocking in 10 or more hours per day and on top of that, were taking shorter breaks.

This was caused because people could not separate work from rest. Since work was home and home was work, everything melted together and people just continued working until they couldn't anymore. This is not a healthy way to live. This is not only limited to those working from home. Sometimes, we can take our work into our rest time. We think that we will just answer one email or finish up a small bit of the project we are working on, and then we end up working for hours more than we should. We have to be able to set definite boundaries for work and rest.

I'm not advocating for completely abandoning your work if you have a deadline to meet or anything like that. If you do have a big project that needs some extra hours to complete, then by all means put in the work. But you should never be working more than what your body is capable of for extended amounts of time. Remember that you are not a robot and your body and mind need to rest.

The only way you will be able to properly switch off from work is if you block everything that is work related when you move into your rest time. So, when it is time to end the work day, switch off. That means cutting off all notifications, calls, emails, and shutting down your laptop. When you completely disconnect you are giving yourself some time to rest so that you are rejuvenated. Then you will be able to give your tasks your best the next day.

Read Emails Once

If you are the type to read an email and get back to it later, you should know that this is hurting your productivity. Essentially, you are using twice the amount of time and energy on that email if you decide to get back to it later. Eventually, you will have so many emails waiting for your attention that you just won't feel like doing it.

If you read the email, take whatever action you want to do with it at that moment. You could reply, archive, forward, delete, or perform the action requested. Whatever it is, just don't leave it there for later. This rule should apply to almost everything. If you can do it now, then don't wait till later or else everything will start to pile up.

Write Down Things That Pop Into Your Mind

Often when we are busy with one task, another one will just pop into our minds. Because we are scared to forget it, we leave what we are doing to complete the new task or we will be distracted by the new thought. This means that we are not fully focused on what we are doing or we keep jumping from task to task. Neither of these is ideal.

The way to remedy this is to write down the thought, idea, or task as soon as it pops into your head. The point of this is to get whatever clutter is in your head out. If it is written down you have assured yourself that you will have something to come back to when you have the time to do so. This reassurance will help you to stop thinking about it. You might also find that those thoughts or actions were not actually necessary and you would have saved yourself time by not doing them. You can either take a small notebook around with you to jot down ideas as they pop into your mind or you can do the same on a note taking app.

Prep the Night Before

Most of the time we will know what the next day will look like so it helps if we prepare for it. We are more likely to do things that are difficult if we have already prepped for them. For one, we won't be wasting time getting things ready, and second, when we prep it's like we have signed a contract with ourselves to get that thing done.

So, if you are planning on going to the gym in the morning, make sure your gym bag is packed and your clothes are laid out. This way all you have to do is roll out of bed, change, and go. If you have an event the next day, plan your outfit and anything else you need so when the time comes, it's just a smooth process to get ready. If you are planning on studying in the morning, set out your textbooks and study aids so that you aren't looking for stuff when you actually have to sit down and study. You could also meal prep for the next day so all you have to do is pick up the food and go.

Being prepared creates less resistance to the task you want to get done. Prepping at night is great because it doesn't take a lot of energy and you have already told your brain what to think about once you get out of bed. It saves you a lot of time the next day and saves your brain power for other important decisions that you have to make throughout the day. The less you have to think about the little things the more space and energy you leave to concentrate on the bigger more important things.

Don't Lay in Bed After Your Alarm Rings

I think we are all guilty of this one. Our alarm rings, we reach for our phones to switch it off and then end up scrolling on Instagram or Facebook for the next 30 minutes. This not only wastes time but it slows us down. How we start our mornings sets us up for the rest of the day.

Social media is not the only reason we lay in bed, sometimes we just keep snoozing the alarm. This is also not good and those 10 extra minutes of sleep are not restful. It would mean the same if you were to wake up and get busy. You are usually more groggy when you have snoozed your alarm a few times than if you got out of bed as soon as the alarm rings.

If you set your alarm for a certain time, make sure that you actually wake up at that time. Switch your alarm off and get out of bed. You can place your phone a distance away so that you have to get out of bed to switch it off. Better yet, don't use your phone as an alarm. Just buy an alarm clock or use a smartwatch to wake you up. This way you are not tempted to scroll on your phone when you wake up.

Do a Quick Workout First Thing in the Morning

We should all be aiming to do some sort of exercise during the day. Our bodies need to move and exercise releases feel good hormones. Waking up and doing a quick workout or even just going for a morning walk will wake your body up and you will see how much sharper your mind is. You will also have more energy for the day. It doesn't have to be anything hectic, even a 10 to 15 minutes yoga session will yield many benefits.

Have Your Snacks Ready

Most of us snack while we are working. If we get hungry, it can be difficult to concentrate on what we are doing. Prepare your snacks in advance so that when the munchies hit you have something to nibble on. This will help you to snack on healthy foods and you won't be wasting time thinking about what to eat, making a snack, or popping out to get something.

High sugar snacks can make us feel sluggish after the sugar high goes away. This will affect how productive you are for the rest of the day. Also, since sugar is addictive the more you eat the more you will want. What starts as a chocolate bar will end up being that, a packet of sweets, and a soda. Choose to eat snacks that will fill you up and give you sustained energy. Fruit, popcorn, and nuts are all good options for this.

Drink Your Water

You might be slightly confused as to why water is on a list of productivity hacks. The truth is that most people don't drink nearly enough water. When we are dehydrated we are sluggish, tired, and can sometimes have false hunger. If you are feeling very tired during the day but are getting a good amount of sleep it might be that you are not drinking enough water.

You should try and get in your eight glasses a day. Keeping a bottle of water on your desk, in your line of sight is a great way to make sure you are drinking enough. If it is available you will continue sipping throughout the day. Also try and drink a glass of water before you eat something. Our bodies often mistake dehydration with hunger so you may not even be hungry in the first palace. Once you see how much more alert you are and how much more energy you have from drinking enough water, you won't want to skip out on it.

Chapter 7:

Burnout

Burnout is an extremely common issue in the workforce. In fact, about 50% of people reported that they experienced burnout in 2019 (Cao Ho My, 2019). That is a huge chunk of the workforce that is stressed, fatigued, and emotionally drained, among other things. The sad thing is that burnout does not stay at the workplace, it spills over into every other area of a person's life. Unfortunately, some companies do not offer the right kind of support to people suffering from burnout, so it is down to the individual to make sure that they don't reach that point, or if they are there already—to resolve it.

What is Burnout?

Burnout is a state of complete exhaustion. It shows up mentally, emotionally, and physically. Although most of the cases of burnout are work related, that is not the only area that can cause a person to feel completely burnt out. If you are feeling overwhelmed, emotionally drained, and you feel as though you are just not able to meet the demands placed on you, you might be suffering from burnout or on your way to it.

Eventually, you might lose all motivation for what you are doing.

When burnout occurs in one area it can quickly manifest itself in all other areas of your life. You can't just leave it at what caused it in the first place. Your overall productivity is sapped and you will struggle to do the simplest of tasks. Many people who suffer from burnout no longer desire to do things or try a bit harder. They are simply just drained.

It is okay to have bad days. Days where you feel overwhelmed, underappreciated, or fatigued. These days come for even the best of us. It becomes a major problem when this becomes the story of your life. If you are stuck in this space then you are most likely suffering from burnout and it is time to do something about it. If you catch it early enough, you will be able to resolve the issue and prevent yourself from going through a major breakdown.

Preventing Burnout

Burnout is a real thing that most people will live through at least once in their lives. Once you reach that point, you are so unmotivated and exhausted that you cannot physically do the things that you need to get done. If you are on a journey to becoming more productive then burnout is one of your worst enemies. The best thing you can do for yourself is to prevent this from happening in the first place. The suggestions below will help you with that.

Know Your Limits

We are all humans and that means we have limits. Some people do not like to hear that but it is the truth. We have a limited amount of energy, attention, willpower, and time each day and there is not much that can be done to increase these. The best thing we can do for ourselves is be aware of our limits and not push ourselves over that.

There might be cases where you have to pull an all-nighter or force yourself to focus for longer than you normally would so that you can meet a deadline, but this should never be the norm. Your limits should be set before you start working. Decide how much you have to give and are comfortable dedicating to work and do your best to stay within those parameters. It might take some experimenting to figure out your limits, but it will definitely help you in the long run.

Learn to Say No

The danger of being someone who gets stuff done is that other people will notice and will want to give you more to do. As much as you may be able to do the work or you may want to help them, it just may not be good for you. You still need time for the other commitments in your life so keep that in mind when you take on something new.

You can say no to anything you don't want to do, even if it's your boss that's asking. In this case, you will have to be respectful in the way you bring it across, saying something like, "I would be happy to take on this task but it does mean that the current project I am working on will take a backseat, would that work for you?" This way your boss has a choice about which is more important to them and you are not trying to fit in a ridiculous amount of work in a short timeframe.

Schedule Time to Do Nothing

We have spoken about scheduling your day and your activities so you know what you need to get done. A common problem with this is that many people pack their schedules so much that there is no time that is not taken up by something. When your schedule is so full there is no wiggle room for tasks that may take a bit longer or for unexpected distractions. This makes it even harder for you to reach the goals for the day.

Even if you end up finishing all the tasks in the right amount of time, the time set out to do nothing can actually be used for that. You could use it to relax and clear your mind or you could do something you enjoy. There is no joy in a day that is filled with tasks from the moment you wake up to the moment you go back to bed.

Make Sure You Are Having Fun and Resting

We don't often associate having fun to being productive but fun plays a vital role in productivity. If we don't take the time to have some fun every once in a while, we will definitely burn out. Our bodies and minds can only take so much before it needs a break. You will enjoy your work so much more if you allow yourself to take a step back from it and work on a hobby or do an enjoyable leisure activity. You will find that when you take a step back to rest and enjoy your time, you will come back to work with a fresh mindset. Your creativity and drive will increase and ultimately, that will make you more productive.

We all need time to let loose and just do the things we enjoy. Humans were not designed to work all day. If you find yourself not enjoying your life or never doing the things that bring you happiness, then you need to reevaluate how you are spending your time. Even if you have to make a commitment and schedule in a time for fun and rest, do that. Just make sure that you get that time for yourself.

Listen to the People Around You

Your loved ones will often be the first people to pick up that you are reaching burnout. If your friends and family are expressing concern about something then it is best to at least hear them out. Even if they are complaining that they never see you anymore, you've missed many get-togethers, or that you are always busy when you are at home. These are all things that indicate that you are not prioritizing your time properly. Remember that your friends and family are the ones that care for you the most so what they have to say really does matter, even if you don't like to hear it.

Resolving Burnout

Maybe you caught it too late, were unable to prevent getting burnt out and now are stuck in the middle of a burnout. As horrible as you may feel now, there are things you can do to get out of a burnout. You can come out of this and be better than before. All you have to do is focus on the right things and take the appropriate steps.

Take a Break

Rest is essential and during this time you have probably not been getting any. We often underestimate how much we need to rest so we push ourselves to the limits and our bodies just can't handle it. The best thing you can do for yourself is to take a break, preferably one where you can get away for a few days. You need time to rejuvenate and time separate yourself from the situation so you can think clearly.

This is not going to solve any of the problems that have caused the burnout but it will help you deal with them better when you get back. If you have the option to take a proper vacation for a few days then do that. Take some time to relax and take care of yourself. Once you are in a better mental headspace you can tackle this in the right way.

Focus on Your Health

If you are going through burnout you are probably not taking care of your health. This can actually worsen your burnout situation. Eating right, exercise, and sleep are usually the first things we throw out the window when we are under a lot of stress. It is definitely not a good idea because these things are what help us deal with our stress. However, I think we have all been there, where we can't be bothered to think about being healthy because of the mountain of work in front of us.

It is time to take back control over your health. If you are not taking care of yourself then you will not be able to deal with the situations around you. I cannot stress how important it is to take care of your body. It is incredibly difficult to feel up to dealing with the issues you are facing if you physically do not have the energy to do so.

Your physical health goes hand in hand with your mental health. You can improve your mental health by actually consciously taking care of your body, so don't brush off this step. Take a look at the food you are eating and remove anything that you know is not good for you. Get your body moving and please get a good night's rest. All the tips for doing these things have already been mentioned in this book so you know how.

Reframe Your Work and Priorities

The easiest solution is to quit your job and find another one where you are treated better and one where you truly love what you do. Unfortunately, this is easier said than done. Sometimes you do not have that option so you need to find other ways around it. I will say that if leaving and finding a better job is an option for you, then by all means do it. If not, then there is some work to be done.

You need to take a look at your job and your work environment and do an analysis. If you are ever going to get back on the horse and start doing your job properly again, you are going to have to find something you love about it. It doesn't even have to be about the work itself. Do you love your co-workers? Do you love what the company stands for? Maybe you get free coffee at lunch time. Whatever it is, you should learn to appreciate the things that can be appreciated. Everything has some good in it if you look for it.

Next you have to know that work is not everything in life. There are other important factors. This means that work does not have to be the place where you get your true satisfaction or where you feel fulfilled. You can get this from another area in your life. This is how you balance out a job or another aspect of your life that you don't particularly enjoy. Find a hobby, side hustle, club, or group that you can find purpose in. Do something you love and put your passion into that.

You are the only one who is in control of you, so if you feel like your world is out of control, it is time to set boundaries. Don't be afraid to tell your boss or manager about your burnout. They need to be aware that the workload you are dealing with is too much. If they are reasonable they will look for ways to lighten the load but you will never know unless you ask.

Remember that you are your priority. You have to do what is good for you and what is good for you is to rest. If your work is taking all of your energy, you should take time away to rejuvenate yourself. Don't overwork yourself, take your leave days when necessary. If you ever feel yourself getting to a point of burnout again, catch it early and take action. You will be amazed at how much of a difference just stepping back for a few days will make.

Chapter 8:

Building Habits That Last

Habits are very important. Our brain wants to save space so it creates neural pathways so that we don't have to pay attention to certain things we are doing. Think about the habits that you currently have in your life. I'm sure you run through the step by step processes of oral hygiene when you brush your teeth in the morning. You barely think about it and can actually use that time to think about other, more important things. If you are someone who drives a specific route often, chances are you don't even think about it. You just get in your car and go, your mind can be preoccupied with other things and before you know it you are at your destination. The brain does this so that it uses up less power for the tasks that you do all the time and has more energy to deal with other, more difficult things.

This is both good and bad. It is good because it gives you energy to think about other things while having good habits in place that take care of the rest. It is bad because if we form bad habits, those can take over our lives without us even knowing about it. This means that we can fall into patterns that hurt our productivity, health, and wellbeing, just because we have fallen into a bad habit. On the flip side, it means that we can actually set ourselves up for success without actively doing any work. The brain is a powerful thing, we just have to use it to our advantage.

It is our responsibility to create good habits and break the bad ones. Nobody else can do it for us. In this chapter, I want to go through ways that we can actually build useful and productive habits and break the bad ones. Remember that habits take time to form so if you think that this is going to be a quick fix, you are going to have to change that mindset. There is definitely going to be some conscious effort from your part before you can let your brain fly on autopilot.

Steps to Building Long-Term Habits

When you set out to build habits, you want them to last for the long term. There is no point in putting in the effort in building a habit if you don't plan on seeing it through. Habits account for about 40% of your daily actions. That's a lot of actions that you are not making a conscious effort to complete. This just shows you how important it is to have good habits that can push you forward. The following steps can be used with any habit you want to build up.

Decide What Habits You Want to Build

Before you can build good habits, you have to decide what habits you want to build. We all have areas in our lives that we want to improve on. The main areas are relationships, health, and work, but if there is another area you would like to work on that's perfectly fine. Choose one of these areas where you feel as though you could use a boost. Usually, you can tell which area you need to work on the most when you look at the bad habits you have. If you have a bad habit in a specific area, this is the perfect place to start building a good habit.

Break Your Bad Habits

Bad habits are often formed without us even knowing. It is just something we do due to the circumstances. Often, we build these habits when we are stressed out, bored, or are being influenced by the wrong people. These are the main catalysts to a bad habit. We all have bad habits, so it is nothing to be ashamed of, but it is something that you have to work on. If you don't think you have bad habits, maybe ask your friends and family to help you pick them out. I'm sure they will have a longer list than you think. Often, the people around you will pick up on these things before you even notice it.

We don't just form a bad habit because we feel like it. They do provide some sort of benefit to us, otherwise, we would not do it. The problem is that the lasting negative effects outweigh whatever short-term benefit it has. For instance, someone will start smoking as a way to cope with stress at work. The short-term benefit is that it calms his nerves and gives them something else to focus on for a short time. In the long-term, it is hurting his health and costing him money that he could be using for something more beneficial.

In order to break a bad habit you need to know where it stems from and why you started it in the first place. The reason being is that bad habits can't just be broken, they have to be replaced with something else. If you know why you started the bad habit, you will know how to replace it. The smoker above would need to find another way to cope and deal with his stress. Perhaps he could chew some gum or try some breathing exercises when he feels the urge to smoke. Simply just not smoking will not help him to stop because he still has to deal with his stress somehow.

When breaking a bad habit, remember to remove as many triggers as possible. You need to make reverting back to the bad habit as difficult as possible. Creating resistance between you and that bad habit is the best way to do that. Having accountability is also a great way to break a bad habit. Pick someone who will walk the journey with you. Tell them the bad habit you are breaking and the good one you are replacing it with. If you do end up failing and reverting back to the bad habit, don't beat yourself up and most importantly, don't give up. A slip-up is to be expected, especially when breaking a habit you have had for a very long time. So cut yourself some slack, tell your accountability partner, and get back on the horse.

The next few steps will just be about building a good habit. You can use them to build the good habit that you are using to break the bad one. These two things will be working simultaneously. Once you have formed your good habit you will know that you have broken the bad one.

Start Small and Build From There

People often struggle to form good habits because they want to do a complete 180 in a short amount of time. The truth is that you cannot build anything that will last if you rush it. Sustainability is your goal, not speed. To build a habit properly, you have to start extremely small, maybe even to the point where it doesn't feel like you are actually changing anything. And that might be true. At the beginning, you will probably not be making any drastic changes in your life but that is okay. The goal is to get started at a sustainable pace and build a system that can easily be increased upon.

For instance, if you want to start exercising, you could enroll in a gym and start doing the circuit for one hour a day. If you were to do that, how long do you think you would last? My guess is that you have actually tried doing something similar and you gave up a few days into it. This is because it was too much of a change. You can't jump from sitting on a couch every afternoon to being a gym enthusiast overnight. Going to the gym might be the actual habit that you want to build but you have to choose a smaller habit that will lead up to that to start with. First, start with doing something physical every day. Try doing five squats every morning. I know this might sound like it isn't going to make a difference, and you will probably not see a difference in your fitness level, but you are creating the habit of moving. When you feel too lazy to get up and do those squats, you can always find the motivation to do five of them because it only takes 30 seconds. This small habit will become the cornerstone to your bigger habit.

As you get comfortable with your small habit, you can increase it. With regards to the exercising example, you can add in a few more squats or maybe add another type of exercise like sit-ups. Next you could try actually leaving your house to exercise. Go for a walk or a jog. Once you have got that down, you could try getting in your car and driving to the gym but only do a short, simple workout. Eventually, you will be so used to the routine of getting out and going to the gym for a few minutes that you will be able to increase the time so that you can get a proper full-body workout. If at any point you feel like you are not motivated enough to do the step you are on, go back to a previous one. Doing something is much better than just throwing the whole thing out and not exercising at all.

Be Consistent

The more you do something the less you will have to think about it. If you don't have to actively think about doing the action, you won't have to motivate yourself to do it. This is the beauty of consistency. You will eventually just fall into step with the routine of it that it will feel weird *not* doing it.

Choose to build your habit at the same time, on the same days. Our brains love routine. You can use this to your advantage. Even if you do not like the action, you will do it because it is part of a routine you have built. If you eat at the exact same time every day, you will almost always feel hungry at that time. If you set your alarm to wake up at the same time every morning, eventually your body will wake up at that time on its own (sometimes regardless of the amount of sleep you got). This is the same kind of effect you want to create with the habit you are trying to build.

The Two-Day Rule

No matter how committed you are or how much you want to build this new habit, you will probably slip up at some point. There will be a day or two where something will come up that will completely throw you off track and you will miss out on building your habit on that day. Life happens and sometimes you mess up. The important thing is that you do not develop a "screw it" attitude.

What I mean is that when you miss a day, don't automatically go, "screw it! I'm not even going to try anymore." This is the worst thing you can do. Many people do this when they are trying to form a habit because they believe that if you break the chain that you will have to start all the way from the beginning. This is not true. All you have to do is pick up from where you left off.

The two-day rule is basically saying that you can skip one day but you are not allowed to miss two consecutive days. If you go into your habit forming with attitude, it becomes a lot more manageable. You have some mess-up room and that means you won't feel like all your hard work was for nothing if you do end up skipping a day.

Make sure you are tracking your habits. This is the only way to be sure that you are not skipping days and it keeps you accountable to yourself. Using a calendar is a great way to track your habits. Every day you perform the habit, color that day in green, place a star on it, or simply check the day off. If you miss a day, color it in red or cross it off with an X. This way, you will be able to see how many days you missed over the course of the month and can aim to do better the next month. If you are a competitive person, this is a great way to compete against yourself and keep yourself motivated. You could also reward yourself at the end of a week where you didn't miss a day. Your reward can be anything as long as it does not go against the habit you are trying to form.

A Few Helpful Tips

If you need a little bit more help to build the right habits, these tips will definitely get you there. During the journey you will probably feel unmotivated at some point, and these tips can help pull you out of that. Read through them so that when the time comes, you will have the knowledge you need to beat a slump. You can also keep these in mind from the start to make the journey towards better habits easier and more manageable for you.

Start With One Habit

It might be tempting to want to break every bad habit and start building all the good ones, but doing too much can stunt your progress. The problem with habits is that you won't see immediate results the day you start trying to build them. This means that it is incredibly difficult to keep motivated if you are trying to change so many things. It is unsustainable to try and do an extreme makeover on yourself in a short space of time.

The solution is to just pick one habit that you want to build or want to break. No matter how much you want to choose, sit down and decide on one. You will probably still feel unmotivated and not want to change the habit anymore but it is much easier to build one habit than to try and build five. You can always find some way to motivate yourself to do one small task.

Find a Role Model

There are probably plenty of people out there that are masters at the habit you are trying to form. It doesn't have to be someone you know personally, just someone who has already achieved the goal you are aiming for. Watch their YouTube videos, read their blog, or listen to their podcasts. Having that person in mind will show you what you are working towards and what you could become if you stick with it. It is a great way to stay motivated and get tips and tricks that will help you along your journey.

Know Your Why

As you continue with this habit-forming process you could eventually start forgetting why you are doing it in the first place. This could easily lead to you being demotivated and not understanding why this is worth the effort. This is the ideal place to remember why you wanted to form this habit in the first place. The end goal is worth the effort put in to get there.

Take some time to write out your why. You can put little reminders everywhere to keep you motivated. Write it out on post-it notes, set up a reminder on your phone, whatever will help you to remember the reason you wanted to change your habits. When things are written down it almost seems more real, it is not the same to have it in your head. Think of it as being accountable to yourself. You can read it back and it is something tangible to keep you motivated.

Conclusion

There was a lot that was covered in this book. You probably have a few things that you can now implement into your life. The goal is not for you to do everything suggested, but to find the things that work for you. Look at your own life and see how you can improve your productivity by implementing the things that resonate with you. Any small change is a step in the right direction. If you look back on your journey and see that you have made some progress, you have something to be proud of.

The worst thing you could do is try and do too much. This is a process and all you need to do is be willing to make small steps. Try implementing one or two of the ideas from this book. Once you are comfortable with those, try a few more. If you try and do too many things too quickly, it won't be sustainable and you might lose motivation. It is not a race. You want these changes to stick for the long-term.

Now that you have gone through the entire book, I want you to go back to the sections that impacted you the most or you feel you need to implement. Write down the things that stood out to you and see what changes you can make based on what you have written down. Start somewhere and start soon. The longer you wait, the more motivation you will need to get going. You have already started the process by finishing this book, so carry on with that momentum.

This book was written to incite real change in the lives of those who read it. Unfortunately, I can't make the changes for you. You have the tools that you need, all you need to do is use them. I know that you will be able to become the most productive person you can be based on the fact that you had the motivation to get the information you need. Remember to be kind to yourself, do what you can, and continue bettering yourself.

References

Akers, W. (2019, November 20). *Is dopamine fasting a way to fix your brain or just a fad?* Healthline. https://www.healthline.com/health-news/what-is-dopamine-fasting#The-science-behind-dopamine-fasting

Brooks, A. (2020, August 12). *19 Productivity Hacks to Get More Done in 2020.* TrueNorth. https://www.ventureharbour.com/productivity-hacks/

Cao Ho My, G. (2019, December 16). *2019 burnout quick stats – 3 things to continue in 2020.* Thrive Global. https://thriveglobal.com/stories/2019-burnout-quick-stats-3-things-to-continue-in-2020/

Chua, C. (2010, June 3). *11 Practical Ways To Stop Procrastination.* Lifehack. https://www.lifehack.org/articles/featured/11-practical-ways-to-stop-procrastination.html

Clear, J. (n.d.). *How to build new habits: This is your strategy guide.* James Clear. https://jamesclear.com/habit-guide

Dizon, J. (2020, April 6). *15 Best Productivity Hacks for Procrastinators.* Lifehack. https://www.lifehack.org/articles/productivity/15-productivity-hacks-for-procrastinators-2.html

Foroux, D. (n.d.). *What Is Productivity? A Definition & Proven Ways To Improve It.* Darius Foroux. https://dariusforoux.com/what-is-productivity/

HelpGuide. (2020, October). *Burnout prevention and treatment.* HelpGuide. https://www.helpguide.org/articles/stress/burnout-prevention-and-recovery.htm#:~:text=Burnout%20is%20a%20state%20of

Instructables. (2012, November 11). *Building a Model Rocket - Introduction.* Instructables. https://www.instructables.com/Building-a-Model-Rocket-Introduction/

Joiner, B. (2018, February 6). *The 5 productive morning routines of highly effective people.* Trello. https://blog.trello.com/best-productive-morning-routines

Kogan, N. (n.d.). *5 tiny productivity hacks that will change your life.* Happier. https://www.happier.com/blog/how-to-be-more-productive-hacks/

Lu, L. (2016, December 9). *8 Ways to Prevent Ruining Your Productivity.* Zippia For Employers.

https://www.zippia.com/employer/8-ways-to-prevent-ruining-your-productivity/

McKay, B., & McKay, K. (2014, January 21). *Attention, please! What every man ought to know about focus.* The Art of Manliness. https://www.artofmanliness.com/articles/attention-please-what-every-man-ought-to-know-about-focus/

Milk, L. (n.d.). *Should You Manage Your Time or Your Energy?* Scoro. https://www.scoro.com/blog/time-and-energy-management/

Ramos, K. (2019, February 19). *10 evening routines that will make you productive at work and life.* Medium. https://medium.com/the-mission/10-evening-routines-that-will-make-you-productive-at-work-and-life-27b596ce8a64

Riddle, J. (2020, November 4). *What is Personal Productivity?* Workawesome. http://workawesome.com/productivity/personal-productivity/#:~:text=Simply%20put%2C%20personal%20productivity%20is

Stretch, R. (2016, March 15). *How to Avoid the 9 Things That Hurt Productivity Most.* Zapier. https://zapier.com/blog/avoid-productivity-killers/

Thomas, M. (2018, March 15). *To Control Your Life, Control What You Pay Attention To.* Harvard

Business Review. https://hbr.org/2018/03/to-control-your-life-control-what-you-pay-attention-to

Thomson, S. (n.d.). *7 Tips to Make Your Afternoons as Productive as Mornings.* Lifehack. https://www.lifehack.org/487395/7-tips-to-make-your-afternoons-as-productive-as-mornings

Thrive Global. (2019, March 27). *Why Managing Your Energy is Key to Maximise Your Productivity.* Thrive Global. https://thriveglobal.com/stories/why-managing-your-energy-is-key-to-maximise-your-productivity/

Timely. (2020, May 21). *How to manage your attention.* Memory. https://memory.ai/timely-blog/managing-your-attention

Widrich, L. (2013, March 26). *The 4 Elements of Physical Energy and How to Master Them.* Buffer Resources. https://buffer.com/resources/the-4-elements-of-physical-energy-on-how-to-master-them/

www.ingramcontent.com/pod-product-compliance
Lightning Source LLC
Chambersburg PA
CBHW050008230526
45465CB00003BB/1310